The Reverend Marga░░░░░░░░░░░░░░░░
Somerset but has live░░░░░░░░░░░░░░░░
since early childhood. S░░░░░░░░░░░░░░
the staff of St James' Church, Selby, in North Yorkshire, and was ordained deacon in 1987 and priest
in 1994. She is Broadcasting Officer for the diocese
of York and broadcasts frequently both locally and
nationally. She has contributed regularly to BBC
Radio 2's *Pause for Thought* and from 1979 to 1990
was Anglican adviser to Yorkshire Television.

Northern Lights

Margaret Cundiff

For Maureen

Sorry you couldn't
be in Bournemouth
hope you enjoy
the book!

Margaret Cundiff

TRIANGLE

First published in Great Britain in 1997
Triangle
SPCK
Holy Trinity Church
Marylebone Road
London NW1 4DU

ACKNOWLEDGEMENTS
Bible quotations are from:
The Good News Bible, published by
The Bible Societies/HarperCollins
Publishers Ltd UK © American Bible Society,
1966, 1971, 1976, 1992.
(Abbreviated as GNB.)
The Revised Standard Version of the Bible © 1952 and 1971.
(Abbreviated as RSV.)

The author and publisher would like to thank the
following for permission to use material in this book:
Mrs Nicolete Gray and The Society of Authors on behalf of
the Laurence Binyon Estate ('For the Fallen', Laurence Binyon);
Stainer & Bell Ltd ('For the Fruits of his Creation'
('Harvest Hymn'), Fred Pratt Green, 1970); ('When I
Needed a Neighbour', Sydney Carter, in *Green Print for
Song*, 1965); The Central Board of Finance of the Church
of England (The Alternative Service Book, 1980);
AP Watt on behalf of The Royal Literary Fund ('How Far
is it to Bethlehem', Francis Chesterton).

British Library Cataloguing in Publication Data
A catalogue record for this book is available from the
British Library.
ISBN 0-281-05002-3

Typeset by Dorwyn Ltd, Rowlands Castle, Hants
Printed in Great Britain by BPC Paperbacks Ltd

*For North Country men and women everywhere,
and all who care to join us!*

ACKNOWLEDGEMENTS

My grateful thanks to all who have contributed knowingly and unknowingly to this book. Special thanks to my family who have again put up with my hammering away at the typewriter all hours and particularly to my husband Peter for his unfailing love and support in every way. To my former editors at SPCK, Myrtle Powley and Rachel Boulding, who guided me and encouraged me in writing, and to Naomi Starkey, my present editor, who has enabled book number ten in the Triangle series to come to birth. To Dr David Hope for his kind comments in the Foreword. Also to all at St James Church, Selby, especially my Vicar, colleague and friend, David Woollard, for the joy of shared friendship and ministry, I owe them more than I can ever express. For Fran and Ian, who have worked so hard and cheerfully to translate my typing into a manuscript. Above all, the Lord's name be praised for all his good gifts, through every season of my life, and in the sure and certain hope that the best is yet to be!

MARGARET CUNDIFF

FOREWORD

Margaret Cundiff has the extraordinary ability to transform each event and circumstance into a rich reflection on the work and power of God in our lives. Whether it be from the pulpit of Westminster Abbey addressing Brownies, on a housing estate in Doncaster, conducting a retreat for ordinands at Ampleforth Abbey or in the setting of her own parish and ministry, Margaret Cundiff, in her own inimitable way and style, at once both homely and lofty, probes beneath the tragic and the comic and the very ordinary to discern the deeper things of the Spirit. Who else, for example, could make something out of frozen Yorkshire puddings?

Margaret Cundiff's style is straightforward and no nonsense – always readable and accessible, and with narrative passages which make it seem as if she really is present addressing you personally and sharing with you something of herself and her own experience and insight into how God has been with her and bought her thus far; the same God who is the God who has come among us and alongside us in Christ.

Here is an immensely attractive and compelling set of reflections and prayers which will surely encourage any reader not only in finding faith but also in further nurturing and deeping faith, and in the awareness that God's presence is everywhere to be perceived and discovered.

David Hope,
Archbishop of York

INTRODUCTION

I had been preaching at a church in the Midlands, and we had reached the 'tea and refreshments in the Church Hall afterwards' stage when a lady from the other side of the hall dashed through the crowd, flung her arms around my neck and said, 'It's wonderful to meet a fellow Yorkshirewoman – as soon as you opened your mouth I felt I was back home in Shipley!' I had to confess to her that I was not a Yorkshirewoman – nor even a Northerner, but born in the West Country, of generations of West Country stock on my mother's side, and Warwickshire on my father's. I spent my childhood in Cheshire, studied in Oxford, worked in Wolverhampton, Nottingham, Manchester and Bolton. Married to a Cheshire man, we made our first home in Bury, Lancashire, where our son was born, then moved back to Cheshire. Our daughter was born in a Manchester hospital and after then, and only then, we moved to 'God's own county' of Yorkshire in 1970.

So where do I belong? The West Country tugs at my heart strings. I was born only yards from the sea – my mother always delighted to tell me she could hear the waves breaking on the shore as I was coming into the world. I have a deep and abiding passion for the sea, so maybe that accounts for it. My grandparents' home was in the beautiful village of Dunster where I spent my first years, and all my holidays. I remember my mother's soft West Country burr which she never lost until the day she died, traces of which some have detected in my own voice; I find overwhelming pleasure in returning to visit the area around Dunster and Minehead. I recall standing by the harbour several years ago at Minehead looking out at the glorious view, and someone beside me remarking 'Isn't it marvellous! Have you been here before?' I proudly replied, 'Been here? I was born here!' So the West Country will always be a magical magnet, drawing me back, and all my memories are precious and lovely of the people, the places, for ever in my heart.

Yet the North has been my life for the greater part of it. We are a Northern family, my husband Peter a devoted Cheshire man, a Maxonian, who returns as often as possible, still retaining his membership of 'The Old Boys' of the Kings School, and of the Macclesfield Field Club. My parents happily settled in Cheshire, firstly in Congleton and then for nearly fifty years in the delightful village of Gawsworth. We were married in the village church of St James; my mother's funeral took place there, prior to her ashes being taken to her beloved Dunster, and my father still enjoys living in the village, now one of the oldest residents, and still very active. Our frequent journeys to see family and friends mean we know every inch of the road from our home in Yorkshire through Derbyshire into Cheshire, but 'home' for me can only mean one place, Yorkshire. I may not have been born and bred in the county but I am well and truly adopted into everything Yorkshire, and to be mistaken for a genuine Yorkshirewoman I take as the highest compliment.

The prospect of moving to Yorkshire all those years ago was not something I looked forward to, for I had heard so many stories about this county designed to put me off, not least that I would never be accepted as 'one of them'. I was also told – by non-Yorkshire people of course – that Yorkshire folk were proud and arrogant, considering everything in Yorkshire was bigger, better and brighter than anywhere else. I soon discovered that it is the most wonderfully comprehensive county with hills and dales, sea and moorland, bustling market towns, go-ahead cities, with tiny hidden jewels of vill-ages, abbeys, castles – you name it, we have got it. And the people? Well, they are proud, in the nicest possible way, loyal, humorous and welcoming. As for being ac-cepted, I have never felt a stranger for I took as my maxim 'If you can't beat 'em, join 'em!' – and when after several years I was invited to join the Radio Leeds 'God-squad' and referred to as 'our lass in Selby' I knew I had arrived! I lost my heart to Yorkshire and here it stays! We have made our home here, brought up our children here, and my ministry is here. It was here God recalled me to the ministry, and brought me step by step to this present day. He knew I would need all the love and support possible, so I reckon that is why he brought me here, because he knew he could rely on the people of York-shire, and especially of St James' Church, Selby to take good care of me, to knock me into shape and keep my feet on the ground. I am not allowed to get self-satisfied, but am constantly forced to 'drive by the seat of my pants' and depend on the Lord's grace and power to fulfil my calling.

They have proved to be faithful, loving friends and guides, my 'northern lights'. They have prayed with and for me, laughed and cried with me, consoled me and celebrated with me. They have led me, pushed me, carr-ied me, and never complained when they appeared in sermons, talks, radio programmes or books. You will meet many of them in this book, and share my experi-ences with the people and places of the north. You will also come further afield with me, particularly to Israel, the Holy Land, and share in my reflections, in words from Scripture and other writings and prayers. We will travel through the changing seasons, through springtime to summer, from autumn into winter, and the festivals along the way, discovering the faithfulness of God in them all, a view of life and eternity lit by northern lights.

A TOUCH OF SPRING

The sun had been trying its best all morning to push through the watery grey cloud, and then suddenly there it was, touching everything with shafts of golden sunlight. 'That's it' I said to myself, and pushing to one side the papers I had been sorting through I put on my anorak and gloves and went into the garage and got my bicycle out. The air felt cold, but as I cycled down the lane I warmed up, and it was good to be out, enjoying the sunshine. There was no doubt about it, spring was here at last, and hopefully to stay. It had been a long hard winter, but now there was the promise of better weather ahead. Already the days were lengthening just that little bit each day, enough to make a noticeable difference.

I stopped to look at the trees and bushes at the end of the lane, and realized, to my delight, that the 'pussy willow' was already showing those tight grey buds, and nearby the catkins were waving their tails merrily – they seemed to know it was spring too. At my feet there were the fresh green shoots which I had not noticed a couple of days earlier, and looking into the wood I saw a furry grey streak of lightning, as a rabbit hurtled back into its hiding place. When I arrived back home I was full of the joys of spring, literally, and insisted Peter came into the garden to see what we could find there. Everywhere there were signs of spring: the mint was pushing through, buds and shoots in the nooks and crannies. Once again God had kept his promise, the seasons would succeed each other, springtime and harvest, summer and winter, all part of his plan, all part of his gift of creation.

Signs of hope – signs of encouragement, the promise for the future. Thank God for them. They are to be seen not just in creation but in human life and experience. The divine spark in creation, in all life, is always there, even when it is frail, small, hidden, unnoticed, and it will never be extinguished, as the prophet Isaiah reminds us: 'He will not break off a bent reed, or put out a flickering lamp' (Isaiah 42.3 GNB). This is a promise that comes home to me when on occasions I may be feeling a little fragile, bent and spent, and then know the gentle but firm hand of God healing and remaking me, enabling me to stand and see straight. The breath of his Holy Spirit fans the flickering flame of faith, hope and love. He does it through people too. It may be a letter that drops on the mat, a phone call or casual conversation, and those words are clearly God reaching out to me. I see myself as a very practical, down-to-earth sort of person, not given to reading into things something more than was intended, but I have learned to recognize God's signature!

It was on such a day in early spring I received a letter from Helen who had written to me several years before telling me that through reading one of my books she had been led back into the Church, but she still had a lot of questions, and was wondering how to step out in faith. I had answered her letter, but never heard from her again until that morning, a letter full of joy, telling of the wonderful things that had happened during the last three years, including graduation, a fulfilling job, marriage and being accepted into the Church. I had encouraged her to keep a journal and she sent me several extracts, which included this one: 'True faith is like a pilot light. It burns when it is warm, unnoticed, but when we are cold and in need of comfort, it lights the flame that keeps us warm. If, perchance your pilot light blows out, it can be re-ignited with love and belief, so it can burn forever in the depth of our soul until we need a bigger flame to guide us home.'

As I read that I knew it was for me. I could have danced down the road, but instead decided a ride on my purple bicycle with its smiley red bell was more appropriate!

As an honorary Chaplain at York Minster a day a month I find so much encouragement in meeting people from all over the world who come and share their stories with me, ask for a blessing, for prayer, for counsel. I am allowed this enormous privilege as I 'loiter with intent' – as is our brief – in that wonderful house of God which is indeed my mother church, as I was ordained Deaconess, Deacon and Priest there, and have shared in so many magnificent occasions which have uplifted and renewed me. Whenever I enter the Minster I am at home. My friends the vergers who look after me so well – where would we be without the vergers! The cheerful policemen, guides, marshals, the staff and the helpers, and the delightful Sisters with their 'And what about a cup of tea?' offers. To see the flower arrangers creating such beautiful and mean-ingful arrangements, and the patient, hardworking cleaners who have such a vital ministry – to me this is all part of worship and praise, all part of a shared ministry, joyfully undertaken in the service of God and his Church by so many, both clergy and laypeo-ple, 'living stones', so that all those who come in may know the touch of God on their lives, find warmth and welcome. York Minster is often described as 'the big-gest umbrella in York' – and sometimes the biggest sunshade too – but it is more, much more than that: a place of refuge, refreshment and renewal, and who knows what effect that has in the lives of the millions who stream in every year. I pray they may find what they need, what they are looking for, even when they cannot express it, but have just felt drawn in by the magnet of all the Minster has been and is.

St James', Selby, my own church, has a much smaller setting than the Minster. Just an ordinary Victorian church, no expensive ornaments, lavish furnishings, ancient artefacts. Set 'around the corner' in a small market town and yet with no less a welcome; a ministry from the people of God, drawn here by the magnet of his love, and by his grace reaching out to each other and into the community around. Week by week sharing in the ministry with David my colleague and all the family of the Church, each time I enter this place my heart leaps for joy and excitement because I know that 'The Lord is here, his Spirit is with us'.

People, places, and all that makes up life day by day are here in a part of North Yorkshire, in the city of York, the town of Selby, the village of Camblesforth and home, at the bottom of a quiet road, where it begins and ends, where my pilot light is kept steady, fed by love.

> The winter is over; the rains have stopped;
> in the countryside the flowers are in bloom.
> This is the time for singing.
> (Song of Songs 2.11–12 GNB)

For love in creation,
For heaven restored,
For grace of salvation
O praise ye the Lord!
(H. W. Baker, 1821–1877)

REACH FOR THE STARS

There was such an air of excitement in the crowded Abbey. A 'family' celebration. They had come in their thousands from every part of the country and from overseas to share in the annual Thinking Day and Founders Day Service for Scouts and Guides. Westminster Abbey alone was not big enough to hold them all, so it was a threesome occasion, being held simultaneously at St Margaret's Church, Westminster, The Methodist Central Hall, Westminster and here in Westminster Abbey. It had been a great surprise and an even greater pleasure to be asked to preach at the Service in Westminster Abbey, and now the great day had arrived, and I stood robed and ready to take part in the celebration. Everywhere I could see Guides, Scouts, Brownies, Cubs, Leaders, friends. The colourful Standards and Flags were ready to be processed through the Abbey, and now I could hear the community singing raising the roof already, everyone enjoying the togetherness, the hallmark of the Movement.

As I looked out at the scene, being lifted by it all, I thought back over the years, to the summer of 1939. It was a most dramatic time in the history of our country, when the storm clouds of war hung heavily upon us, with desperate uncertainty about what the future held for anybody. For me, a seven-year-old girl in a small Cheshire village, there was something far more important and life-changing in prospect. Each day during that long summer I pestered my mother with the question, 'How many more days now?' because in the September I was going to join the Brownies. It had been such a long wait, and how I had envied my older friends who wore that exciting brown uniform, yellow tie and woolly hat. Soon now I would be able to wear that uniform, join in the exciting times, work for those wonderful badges, and wear them proudly on my arms for all to see . . . but it did seem such a long time to wait . . .

One morning my parents sat me down, and looking very serious my mother said, 'We have got something to tell you, and you've got to be a very brave girl.' I felt like bursting into tears. Surely after all this time of waiting . . .? 'You see, there's a war on now, our country is at war with Germany, and we don't know what is going to happen.' I hardly dared put my question, but I had to know. 'But will I still be able to join the Brownies?' My mother looked at me dubiously and then said, 'Well, I suppose so.' I breathed a sigh of relief, 'Ah well, that's all right then isn't it?', and off I went. Never mind the war, I was going to be a Brownie!

I did become a Brownie, did wear that wonderful brown uniform, did earn an armful of badges, become a Sixer before becoming a girl in blue, a Guide, and by the end of the war had collected yet more badges and a Patrol Leader's stripes. Later on I turned my attention to the boys, becoming a Cub Leader, and now today no longer wearing a uniform, or being on active service with Scouts and Guides, I still feel a member of the family, for 'once a member, always a member' I believe, and when I am asked to share in any Guiding or Scouting occasion I do so gladly, and with a deep sense of gratitude for all I have received from the movement.

So, in Westminster Abbey that February morning the memories came flooding back, and a sense of 'Who'd have thought it?' In my sermon I told of my

Brownie days, and also of the way God had sustained me through my life, and that he enables us all to be the person he wants us to be, to be adventurous, unafraid, whatever the situation. I quoted some words from the Order of Service, 'We all need a helping hand on our own journey through life. Reach for the stars, but first open your heart to God, for without his help your journey will never be completed.' As I said those words and leaned out of the pulpit, looking at the faces around, I saw her, a Brownie near the front. She was looking up at me, her eyes wide, and I forgot Westminster Abbey, forgot the crowd, even forgot my sermon. I saw in that little girl myself, all those years ago, and I wanted her to know she could do anything with God's help; all she had to do was trust him and 'go for it'. I looked at her, and spoke directly to her 'And that means you! You can do ANYTHING with God's help, you can reach for the stars, swing on them, you can do it, you really can. Do you believe me? It's true!' She smiled back at me, a friendly warm smile of confidence, and then I continued with the sermon, the service went on, and afterwards the crowd dispersed, although we kept meeting up with little groups around the Westminster area as they 'made a day of it'. One of those lovely happy days, days to be savoured, remembered for always.

A few days later I received a letter from Lady Baden-Powell, in which she wrote, '. . . the Brownie you picked out was sitting up there as she had earlier been in floods of tears, so it was a marvellous lift for her . . .' Another letter came, no name or address, just signed 'Yours in Guiding', but it said 'I have never before celebrated Thinking Day at Westminster Abbey. I was sitting in front of the pulpit, and was also enrolled as a Brownie in 1939 . . .'

I often thank God for that day, for the opportunity God gave me to reach out to a little Brownie, just beginning her life in the movement, and to another, who like myself entered those ranks at the beginning of a very uncertain and traumatic time in history, who has discovered like me that life can be full of joy and fulfilment through the adventure of service.

For that Brownie of today life is as much, if not more, uncertain than for us when we began at the end of the 1930s. As we come nearly to the end of the twentieth century who knows what changes lie ahead as we go into the twenty-first? What sort of a world will it be when that Brownie leaves school, goes about the task of finding a job, building her adult life, falling in love maybe, raising her own family? I don't even know her name, where she comes from, or her circumstances; all I know is I saw someone who was open to listen, eager to know, and ready to respond. I hope she will always enjoy being part of the great movement of Guiding and Scouting, help carry it forward into the future, but above all I pray she may come to know and love the One who put the stars in place, who knows each of them by name, who knows her by name, and calls her to 'reach for the stars'; that she may open her heart, her life to him, and so travel through life wisely, well and with joy, and never lose that sense of purpose, that God-given purpose wherever she goes.

Look up at the sky! Who created the stars you see?
The one who leads them out like an army,
he knows how many there are and calls each one by
     name!
His power is so great – not one of them is ever
     missing!
(Isaiah 40.26 GNB)

Father,
thank you for the vision you have set before us
 through creation,
through the life of your Son Jesus Christ,
through the witness of men, women and children
through to this day.
May we too discover the joy of reaching and
 touching the stars,
enabled by your power and love.

DEATH'S DARK SHADOW

The remaining snow clung to the walls and hedge bottoms like limpets to rock, fiercely unyielding. The air was crisp, not the biting cold of the last few weeks but with a cleansing freshness that gave me a feeling of exhilaration, dispelling the sluggishness of body and mind. I walked along the path beside the Guest House of Ampleforth Abbey, and stood looking out across the magnificent Abbey and School, the grounds stretching as far as the eye could see, set amid the glorious North Yorkshire countryside, near the old market town of Helmsley. 'How easy it is to feel peaceful here,' I thought, 'to be able to give oneself totally to God, nothing to disturb the peace, nothing to intrude.'

I had been invited to conduct the annual Retreat of the York Diocesan Fellowship of Vocation – a group of men and women who were exploring their vocation to ministry in the Church of England. For some it was just a vague stirring, a wondering where God might want them to be. For others ordination was already firmly fixed; having gone through the selection procedure they were well on with their college training, some nearing the end with the date of their ordination and the parishes where they were to serve arranged. In charge was the Archbishop of York's Chaplain, who was also Director of Ordinands, David Wilbourne. I had been delighted when he had invited me to conduct the Retreat, although I found it a daunting prospect, especially knowing of the learned and holy people who had been the conductors in previous years. But the invitation was too good to refuse: the prospect of a long weekend at Ampleforth, the opportunities for worship and reflection, seemed to me a gift from heaven. Later on that afternoon as I sat with the group in the Abbey, the haunting sound of plainsong echoing around, it was indeed 'a vision of peace'. I understood how that music had touched so many, topping the charts with recordings made in the Abbey, and I was so grateful to be experiencing it not merely on tape or disc but actually in that place, 'live'. Kindly monks unobtrusively found our places for us in the service books, almost as though they were presenting to us a precious jewel – but then that was exactly it, the precious jewel of God's word set to music. As the monks glided silently into their stalls in the choir I noticed two young monks wheeling in two elderly ones in wheel chairs. As they brought them to their places they knelt down and placed the old men's feet in a comfortable position, and with such expressions of love and respect as they did so that I thought of Jesus washing his disciples' feet, kneeling before them with that same expression of love and respect for those he was serving. I recognized that expression again as we sat down to dinner. A young monk, standing in for the usual Guest Master, said grace, smiled upon us, and with a sweep of his arms said 'Eat!'

'Benedictines are famed for their hospitality' whispered the young man on my right. Hospitality – what a lovely word! It describes the sharing of the deeply precious things and the ordinary everyday with brothers and sisters. We may have been of a different Christian denomination, we may have been strangers, but we were treated as honoured guests. I found this a real challenge, for I have a lot to learn about the true nature of hospitality. How shoddy, half-hearted and paltry seemed my sort of hospitality compared with this – but then I decided it was so much easier for monks in gracious peaceful surroundings to practise hospitality than for those of us who have to cope with being part of a busy, noisy world, with constant interruptions, time-consuming meetings, delays, demands. All right for monks – they had peace on a plate. How would they cope with our lives, I wondered.

We could not know then but before the end of the Retreat we would be brought up sharp by a tragic event. The one who would have been our Guest Master, a monk much loved and valued for his kindness, his care for others, a man with great talent and ability, took his own life in the peaceful wood by the Guest House, and was found dead by one of our group. Suddenly we realized that beauty, music, even faith cannot drown the anguish of the human heart. It is not only in the busy frantic places, the ugly isolation of tower blocks, the grimy sprawl of grey depressing urban decay, the violent inner city areas, that men and women cry out in agony 'No more!' and end their lives, but also in tranquil gentle woodlands, amid beauty, peace, security.

For us the Retreat continued that weekend, amid the grief and confusion. Life went on, the life of Ampleforth, of the monks, of the music. Our life went on. We stuck to our timetable. I gave the addresses, we joined in worship and silence, we sat, we walked, we ate, we thought . . . but in our hearts we were all asking the same question 'Why?' and there came no answer.

After lunch on the Sunday we said our goodbyes and thank yous, and went our separate ways again. I walked along the same path as I had done when I arrived just a couple of days before. I looked out at the same view. At my feet clumps of snowdrops, pure, white, graceful. The daffodils were already turning their heads over, ready to break into a golden carpet, the buds on the trees showing green, everywhere the promise of life, new life. I thought of the monk, with all the promise of life before him walking this path, up into the wood and ending it all – if only . . . Yet we are all fragile human beings, however strong we may appear. We all have deep inner depths, where we harbour fears, failings, disappointments, burdens, and we need to be able to share them with others, allow them to help us, so we can realize we are not alone, we need human help as well as God's help – all of us, otherwise life can prove too much, even for the strongest.

As I drove home through the beautiful rolling countryside, past elegant houses, the dainty villages along the way, I reflected on the weekend. It certainly had not been as I – or any of us – had expected or anticipated. We had all been deeply disturbed and challenged by the tragic event we had been part of. We could not dismiss it and say 'It's not our problem'. It was, and will remain so, it has left its mark on us, indelibly.

That word 'hospitality' surfaced again and again in my mind, and I prayed that through what we had experienced at Ampleforth – the good and the tragic alike – we might have a deeper sense of what hospitality involves, and might seek that true spirit of hospitality so that we might reach out to those who are hungry, aching, tired and weary, whether of body, mind or spirit, and draw them into the safety and security of loving acceptance, genuine warmth and understanding.

Help to carry one another's burdens, and in this way you will obey the law of Christ. (Galatians 6.2 GNB)

When I needed a neighbour were you there, were
   you there?
When I needed a neighbour were you there?
And the creed and the colour and the name won't
   matter, were you there?
(Sydney Carter)

Lord,
so many carry burdens alone, suffer alone, go into
the darkness alone. Yet you have put us here on
earth together, to share, to reach out, to comfort and
encourage one another. Lord help me to hear, help
me to see, help me to reach out with your compassion, your love, with your spirit of hospitality and
acceptance, and help me to do it now.

GIVE THANKS WITH A GRATEFUL HEART

It had been one of those days when nothing seemed to go according to plan – my plan anyway. Already feeling tired and jaded by a heavy week, which had included a number of unexpected problems rearing their ugly heads, I did not feel in the mood to drive nearly 30 miles to speak at a Deanery Lent Course in Doncaster. The route was uninspiring, down the motorway, through an industrial estate and then on to the sprawling conglomeration of housing estates. I stopped to consult my map. I realized I was in the right general direction, but where to go now, I had no idea. Seeing a young man strolling down the road towards me I decided to ask my way. Mentioning the church he frowned, thought a moment, then jerked his thumb behind him. 'Up there, first junction, turn right, then straight on to the next junction, turn left, and you can't miss it.' With that he was gone. 'Can't miss it? – just watch me' I thought. However, following his directions carefully I was relieved to see ahead the outline of a tall grey church, but what surprised me was to see so many people walking purposefully along in the direction of the church. When I got near I could also see people approaching from other directions too, and as I pulled in beside the church I found myself in a traffic jam, cars everywhere, and not a space to be seen. 'Surely they are not all going to church, there must be something else on around here' I decided, as I was forced to travel to the end of the road to find a parking place. As I walked back towards the church I found myself in a queue to get in, and entering the large Victorian building to my amazement I saw that the church was already almost full, and a steady stream still behind me. I felt thrown. I had imagined a small informal meeting in the Church Hall. How on earth was I going to deal with this crowd, all sitting in serried rows? I had come prepared to lead a discussion on the subject 'Your kingdom come, your will be done on earth as it is in heaven'. No way would I be able to have a discussion, it was going to have to be a straight address. I uttered my special prayer for such occasions: 'Help!' and tried to rearrange in my head the material for the evening.

The Rural Dean took me into the vestry, put the fire on and left me to 'get sorted out'. A typical vestry, all the usual paraphernalia around, reminding me of ours at St James', Selby. Photographs and pictures always interest me – you can tell a great deal about a place by the pictures on the wall – and my attention was caught by a large picture depicting the inside of the church, probably from around the turn of the century. I was still gazing at the picture when the door opened and the Vicar, a young man, came in, holding out his hand in welcome. Seeing me looking at the picture he remarked, 'It hasn't changed has it? But we have a scheme for the re-ordering of the church, so we can use the space more profitably. It's so difficult with all those pews.' He enthusiastically went on to describe the plans for the church and for their outreach into the surrounding area. It was evident that there was a real feeling of hope for the future, an expectation of good things to come, a sense of buoyancy, and as I re-entered the church I felt lifted by that same feeling of anticipation, no longer worried about the evening. It was going to be good, I was sure of that. The opening hymn nearly lifted the roof off the church, sung with such enthusiasm, and when I said 'Let's now be quiet for a moment and commend this evening to the Lord' the air was electric and I knew that God was not only going to touch those people, he was going to touch me too. The sense of the Lord's presence was overpowering, there was life, urgency, a real openness. As we came to the end of the evening I asked them to think of something good they had heard or seen or been part of that day – whether an item of news, a conversation, an answered prayer, a letter or phone call, a reading, a joke, a smile, a handshake, something that had brightened their day, brought them close to God or to others – and then I asked them to turn to the person next to them and share it. I leaned back in the pulpit and shut my eyes, and found myself in heaven. I knew I was in heaven because of the angelical music. No, my feet had not left earth, nor had my mind 'blown', but it was the sound of joy being shared, a symphony of voices in harmony, in praise, dancing, twirling, leaping in unending delight. No orchestra, no choir could have produced such a sound. I was loth to bring it to an end, but as I opened my eyes, looked out upon those happy faces, there came an almost audible sigh of contentment, a heavenly 'Amen', in unison.

It was hard to tear myself away afterwards, I was still trying to take it all in. All those people turning out for a Lent Course, the enthusiasm, warmth, wonder, the sheer exhilaration of it all. The journey home seemed so short compared with coming, and the darkness of that winter's evening like a pleasant summer's day. As for feeling tired, I was ready for anything, in fact I sang all the way home! As I turned off the motorway, on my last lap home I burst into singing a hymn written long before that church in Doncaster had been even thought of, before housing estates, industrial complexes or motorways. It was William Cowper's hymn:

Jesus, where'er thy people meet,
There they behold thy mercy seat;

Where'er they seek thee, thou art found,
And every place is hallowed ground.

For thou, within no walls confined,
Inhabitest the humble mind;
Such ever bring thee when they come,
And going, take thee to their home.
(William Cowper, 1731–1800)

Maybe the words were old-fashioned, but the senti-
ment was right up to date. I could vouch for that, for
after all, I had met the Lord that very evening – in
Doncaster – and what was more, He had brought me
safely and joyfully home too!

All you that are righteous,
  shout for joy for what the Lord has done,
  praise him, all you that obey him.
Give thanks to the Lord with harps,
  sing to him with stringed instruments.
Sing a new song to him,
  play the harp with skill, and shout for joy!
The words of the Lord are true,
  and all his works are dependable.
The Lord loves what is righteous and just;
  his constant love fills the earth.
(Psalm 33.1–5 GNB)

Father,
thank you for the unexpected experiences of the joy
of heaven, for the realization of your kingdom here
on earth, in the company of your faithful people.
Give us the confidence to share with others what
you have done for us, always ready to sing your
praises, giving thanks, with grateful hearts.

JUNK OR TREASURE?

There was something wrong with the drawer, it just would not close. However hard I pushed it nothing happened. The only thing was to empty it out, and so get to the root of the trouble. It was like an Aladdin's cave! As I emptied it out on to the floor the pile got bigger and bigger. However had I got so much into one drawer? No wonder it would not shut – it was so full there was no space for the runner to move. I started to wade through the pile. I discovered things I thought I had lost long ago; there were a few useful items, but the majority of it was sheer junk – no other word to describe it, junk. I knew of course how it had all got in there. As I tidied up the room, things lying around had to be found a home, and so I popped them in the drawer, a veritable black hole. Outworn, outdated, discarded bits and pieces, the accumulated junk of years. I knew why I had kept them: 'They might come in', 'It could be useful sometime', or even 'I don't want to part with that'. So the easiest thing had been to stuff them in the drawer, and I had gone on stuffing things in until the drawer could take no more, and resisted! I must admit I had to make myself throw things away that day – it does come hard to break the habit of a lifetime of hoarding. I suppose most of us are guilty of hoarding rubbish, we push it away into cupboards and drawers, 'in the roof', the shed or garage. I know several people who cannot get their cars in their garages because the garage is full of . . . they might say useful articles, but really there is a limit to how many quarter tins of paint, broken toys, old deckchairs and assorted pieces of timber you can keep in one garage isn't there? But then we all do it, apart from the neatest and well-organized people, of which I am not one. So we go on providing homes for mice and other unwelcome visitors, while the junk gathers dust and rust using up space that could well have been more usefully employed. The older generation had the right idea with the yearly 'spring clean', a time set aside for clearing out; but even so, often they could not bear to part with things, and after being given a good shake out, a dust over, most went back in the same place until the next spring.

Human nature, you could say – yes, I suppose it is, but far more dangerous is the mental and spiritual junk we accumulate, allowing it to clutter up our lives and cause very real problems for us and for others. Things like old prejudices, stale misconceptions, outworn resentments, bitter memories, unresolved disagreements, soured relationships. We hang on to them, won't let them go, but of course it would not do to have them on display, so we push them into the back of our minds, the hidden recesses of our lives. But they have a very nasty habit of pushing into the present, overflowing and taking over what is good and useful, until the whole sorry mess brings us to a sudden and unexpected halt, and we wonder how we have got into such a state. It may be at that point, if we are sensible, we stop and take stock, bring it all out into the open, sort it out, and make a fresh start. Sadly these things have a way of creeping back into our lives if we are not careful, if we leave a crack open for them to climb back in. How many times does that happen? When we think we have dealt with something once and for all, it rears its ugly head in another part of our lives. Unlike physical rubbish, the mental and spiritual junk is alive and active, and can multiply at an alarming rate, especially if given food and shelter, and like those verminous creatures who thrive on rubbish it can thrive in the warm and welcoming environment of selfishness, pride and ignorance.

In the Baptism Service of the Church of England there is what we call 'the decision' and the parents and godparents answer both for themselves and on behalf of the children. The same words are also used at the renewal of baptism vows at Confirmation by the candidates, and by others who come to renew their baptismal vows. The question is put: 'Do you turn to Christ?' – the response, 'I turn to Christ'. 'Do you repent of your sins?' They reply 'I repent of my sins'; and finally 'Do you renounce evil?' to which they affirm 'I renounce evil'. These are very powerful promises, and I always put great emphasis on them when I prepare parents for the baptism of their children, explaining 'You are not making these promises to me, or to the Church, but to God, and you must think very hard about whether you can make them, and if you can, whether you will do what you say you will do.' It is an act of faith and will, turning to Christ in repentance, and then, having done with evil, getting rid, throwing it out. But easier said than done, and none of us, with the best will in the world, can do it, but then we don't have to in our own strength. As we make that act of faith, that dedication to action, then Christ is there with us, taking the junk from our hands, our hearts, our lives and disposing of it. We can, by his grace, make a new start, make room for all that is good, beautiful, useful and lovely, although we need to remember that it is possible to go hunting for the junk and bring it back – take warning!

When our lives are emptied of the junk then Christ refills them with his treasures of forgiveness, peace, joy, hope and power. You will not see these displayed on the *Antiques Roadshow*, but they are worth everything – they are priceless and they are free to those who have the desire for them and the available space to receive them.

If we say we have no sin, we deceive ourselves, and the truth is not in us. If we confess our sins, God is faithful and just, and will forgive us our sins and cleanse us from all unrighteousness. (1 John 1.8–9 RSV)

Lord,
I open my life afresh to you,
help me to discard all that hinders my relationship
   with you, and with others,
fill me anew with the treasures of your grace
so I might live to your praise and glory,
now and for always.

THE LORD SAYS 'COME!'

I sat in the chapel at the Retreat House in Chester, enjoying the peace and tranquillity inside, while gazing out through the window into the garden. The rain had stopped, and now the sun had come out, lighting up the drops suspended on trees, flowers and bushes as though they were diamonds. Over to the right I could see the magnificent magnolia tree in the Bishop's garden, next door, shimmering in the early morning sunlight.

I was in Chester as a Selector at a Selection Conference for men and women who were offering for the ministry in the Church of England. In a few minutes I would be joined in the chapel by fellow selectors and candidates for the service of Holy Communion. This morning I was to be the celebrant and so had come down to the chapel early to prepare and reflect. As I sat there I thought of all the other Selection Conferences I had been part of over the years, realizing with a jolt that it was almost half a century since I had been a candidate for lay ministry, and 20 years since my Deaconess Selection Conference. Now I was attending my last Conference as a Selector, having served almost 15 years. 'Where are they now?' I wondered. All those I had met over the years, right from the beginning when as a very naive 19-year-old I had gone full of the confidence of youth to Shallowford House in Staffordshire, and amazingly had been recommended. I must have had a guardian angel watching over me for I would certainly not have recommended someone like me – in fact I would have wondered how such a candidate had been allowed to cross the threshold! I remembered too the joy of my Deaconess Selection Conference at the Royal Foundation of St Katharine in London, the care, the prayer and concern of everyone, knowing the rightness of that step at that time, and again, being recommended. In the early eighties I was invited by the Archbishop of York, Stuart Blanch, to be a Selector, 'poacher turned gamekeeper' you might say, and I had accepted with great joy, realizing the tremendous privilege and responsibility of being a pastoral selector.

In those early years only men could offer for the priesthood in the Church of England. For women it was for lay ministry or as a deaconess, then from 1987 women were admitted as deacons, and finally from 1994 women have had the same opportunity as men to offer for training for the priesthood.

It had been so exciting for me to see men and women candidates offering for training for priesthood at the last Selection Conference I had shared in, just before my own ordination as a priest, but this morning was indeed 'the icing on the cake' – to be the celebrant at this service, to exercise my calling fulfilled – a wonderful reminder, if I needed it, of God's abundant love, the One who had sustained me through the years.

Sitting there in the chapel, the memories reawakened, I thanked God for all those who had helped me on my path through so many years, my selectors, and fellow-selectors, and all those candidates it had been my privilege to meet over my time as a selector: some faces as clear in my mind as the day I had first met them, others a blur, but all part of my life, my journey, as I was of theirs. I glanced down at the list of names I held in my hand of those at this Conference, and as I read through them I prayed for each of them that they might know the strength of the Lord, his love surrounding them as together we explored their calling, and that selectors and candidates alike might have the guidance of the Holy Spirit as we shared together, as decisions were made.

The chapel door opened and Roy, the Conference Secretary from the Advisory Board of Ministry, came in. 'Shall I light the candles now?' he asked. I nodded, and then went into the vestry to robe, ready for the service. Then I looked in the mirror, and saw her. Her fair hair was showing signs of grey, a few wrinkles here and there – or were they laughter lines, I wondered – I hoped so! Neatly dressed, her 'dog collar' showed above her cassock and surplice, and over them the brilliant red stole, marking the celebration of the Holy Spirit, coming with tongues of fire. I smiled at her, and of course she smiled back, for it was me: the girl who had bounced along to that Selection Conference nearly half a century ago, and who had bounced along ever since, celebrating with joy the enabling power of the Holy Spirit, God's steadfastness and love, and who would now share in the deepest possible way with those gathered here today.

I returned to the chapel, the candles shining bright, the Table prepared. I looked at the faces of those gathered there. 'Welcome' I said, and raising my hands in praise and thanksgiving, 'The Lord is here – his Spirit is with us. Alleluia!'

He who calls you will do it, because he is faithful.
(1 Thessalonians 5.24 GNB)

> Jesus, confirm my heart's desire
> To work, and speak, and think for thee;
> Still let me guard the holy fire,
> And still stir up the gift in me.
> (Charles Wesley, 1707–1788)
>
> Thanks be to God!

IS THIS THE PLACE?

It was the stack of wooden crosses that caught my eye. There they were, stood up neatly outside the door of the church. Plain wooden crosses, about six feet high by three feet across. They reminded me of the fire beaters placed at strategic places over the North Yorkshire moors, and in the forest areas, there to be used in case of emergencies. But this was neither moor nor forest but in the heart of the city of Jerusalem, outside the Church of the Holy Sepulchre. I asked our guide what they were for. 'Oh, you can hire them' she told me. 'Pilgrims hire them to walk the Via Dolorosa. Then when they have finished they return them to this point.' I had not thought of people hiring crosses, but come to think about it, where had those processions of pilgrims got their crosses from? I had assumed they had brought them with them. 'Crosses for hire' – somehow it did not seem right, hiring a cross. Was it by the hour, by the day? Did you have to pay a deposit? It all seemed rather commercialized, but then so much of what I had already seen was, and no doubt there was more in store. I had been warned, had expected to meet it, but crosses for hire, that I found odd.

I turned away, to enter the church. It was not an attractive looking building, set in the cramped area of the city, but this was, so the guide told us, 'the most holy place for Christians, where Jesus was crucified, was buried, and from where he rose from the dead'. It was dark and even less appealing than outside, inside the church. A jumble of altars, hangings, icons, the smell of candles, incense. Priests of many Christian denominations were intent in worship in their own portion of the church, and the guide explained they had a rota for taking services at the most holy of places, over the actual site, within the church. We moved around silently from one part to another, and were then taken into a dirty, neglected area, a broken altar in one corner, pieces of wood, stones, discarded items lying around. The guide explained 'This area is claimed by two different Christian groups, but they will not give way to one another, and neither will give permission for the other to use it, to care for it, so no one can do anything here.' She shrugged her shoulders. 'So you see the result, when they cannot agree.' I felt so sad, Christians behaving like that. Why couldn't they come to some agreement? But then, it happens in so many places, not just in Jerusalem. The guide went on, 'But this is nothing to what happens sometimes. They fight amongst themselves, all of them. They think all this church belongs to them, and resent others being here.' I found that a very disquieting statement, but realized the truth of what she was saying.

Then it was on to visit the Holy Sepulchre, joining the slow procession of people from all over the world all wanting to see this holy place, many of them falling on their knees, kissing the stones, there was the mumbling of prayers, and I felt sad, almost depressed. Was it because of what the guide had said about the arguing, was it because I felt no warmth here, no response within me to this place? If this WAS the place, surely I would feel within me a sense of holiness, of awe, and I didn't. It was evident, looking around, that many did; I was touched by their piety, their reverence, their excitement at being in this place, but for me, there was nothing. I thought of those neatly piled crosses outside, and suddenly in my mind I saw another cross, the one in our church at home in Yorkshire. It is about the same size as one of those outside the church in Jerusalem, and during Holy Week it is gradually moved down the church so that it becomes the focal point during the week, the cross coming closer day by day. On Good Friday we gather around it, remembering what happened on the cross, and then on Easter Day the cross is still there, but as a reminder that Jesus is risen. The cross not a sign of death and defeat but of victory, the way to life. As folk make their way to receive Holy Communion, the children for a blessing, they have to come past the cross, the cross behind them, as it was for Jesus. The empty cross, for the Lord is alive, for ever.

As I looked again at the site marked out as the place where Jesus Christ had lain, that stone area, argued over, fought over, disputed, revered, I thought of those who had first come to the tomb, whether it was here, nearby, or wherever, and had found it empty, as empty as this was now, and of what that meant, for them, for millions and millions of people, including me, from that time on – the tomb was empty, because the Lord had risen! The Sepulchre was holy not just because the Lord had been laid to rest in it, but because he had risen from it! 'Not here but risen!' I said aloud, as I turned and left that place, going out into the sunshine again. A photographer stood there, camera slung around his neck. He gave me his card. 'You want photograph here? Memento – I take?' I waved him aside. 'No thank you, not here.' Somehow a posed photograph appealed as little as crosses for hire. As I walked away I thought again of that dark place, still feeling sad it had not done anything for me, but then I realized, of course it had! It had reminded me powerfully again of the fact of the empty cross, the empty tomb, of the Lord of life and his promise 'Because I

31

live, you will live also'. I looked up into the blue, blue sky and felt the warmth of the sun on my face. 'Christ is risen, he is risen indeed, Alleluia!' I sang, and went on my way, rejoicing.

The angel spoke to the women. 'You must not be afraid,' he said. 'I know you are looking for Jesus, who was crucified. He is not here; he has been raised, just as he said. Come here and see the place where he was lying. Go quickly now, and tell his disciples, "He has been raised from death, and now he is going to Galilee ahead of you; there you will see him!" Remember what I have told you.' So they left the tomb in a hurry, afraid and yet filled with joy, and ran to tell his disciples. (Matthew 28.5–8 GNB)

Jesus lives! thy terrors now,
Can, O death, no more appal us;
Jesus lives! by this we know
Thou, O grave, canst not enthral us.
Alleluia!
(C. F. Gellert, 1715–1769,
translated by Frances E. Cox)

Thank you, Lord,
that by your death upon the cross, and your rising again from the dead, we can enter into that new life here on earth, and know the assurance of the joy of all eternity with you in heaven.

WHAT ABOUT THE
CHILDREN?

The door bell rang, and I opened the front door to find half a dozen eight- or nine-year-olds standing there, one with a notebook. 'Looks like they want sponsoring for something, or maybe their ball has gone in our garden' I thought, for they all looked very serious. I recognized them, for they all lived nearby, and went to the local school at the back of our house. 'Mrs Cundiff, do you believe in the devil?' the boy at the front of the group asked. He looked so solemn, and the others looking at me intently, waiting for the answer. I asked them why they wanted to know, but the reply came, 'But is there a devil, Mrs Cundiff?' I tried to explain that there was – they couldn't see him, but he did try to make us do wrong things, although we were not to be afraid of him, or give in to him, because God had sent Jesus to help us fight him, and do the right things. Another boy joined in eagerly, 'Jesus believed in the devil didn't he? Because the devil tempted him when he was in the desert.' 'Do you remember me telling you that when I came into school?' I asked. The boy nodded, and I felt so pleased I had accepted the head teacher's invitation to go into school a couple of times a term and take assembly. It wasn't the school in my own parish, where I went regularly, but the one in the village where we live, and where I am part of the Local Ecumenical Project, sharing with the Methodist Minister and Vicar.

I had been in to the school at the beginning of Lent – hence the story of the temptations of Jesus, but had also been in the week before my young visitors had arrived on my doorstep. It being just before they broke up for the Easter holidays, I had told them of the last days of Jesus, from Palm Sunday through Holy Week to Easter. In describing the Palm Sunday procession into Jerusalem I likened it to the excitement of a football crowd waiting for their team captain coming onto the pitch. All the cheering, shouting, waving of scarves, but for Jesus they waved the palm branches and shouted their praise and welcome. 'What did they shout?' I asked the children. They were quiet – I could see they were thinking hard, but couldn't quite remember the word. 'I'll give you a clue' I said. 'It goes Ho. . . ho. . .' A boy at the back waved excitedly at me. 'I know, I know, it was Ho Gazza!' Trying not to smile, I said 'Well, very close, but it was Hosanna!'

The girl with the notebook looked round at the little group, cleared her throat and then said to me as though making an important announcement, 'Now Mrs Cundiff, I would like to ask you a few questions. It's a project for school.' So that was the purpose of their visit: they had been set a holiday assignment, and I was part of it. 'That's fine, what do you want to know?' The girl licked her pencil, opened the notebook and poised the pencil ready to take down my replies. 'I've got three questions. The first one is, when did you first hear about Jesus? Question two, do you like telling other people about Jesus? Question three, has anyone ever told you something about Jesus you didn't know?' They took quite a time to answer, but the children's interest never flagged. Then the girl said, 'Well, it's not really for a school project, it's for us, we wanted to know' – and with that they turned, waved to me, and ran down the path.

'That was an interesting conversation,' my husband Peter said as I came back into the sitting room. 'They certainly put you on the spot.' Yes, they did, and how glad I was to be put on the spot by them. It was a delight for me to have to give straight answers, to think clearly, and answer truthfully about my own faith and life. I find children are fascinated with the person of Jesus, they really want to know about him, want to find out for themselves, and are not afraid to ask. Yet the sad thing for most children today is, do they get the opportunity? I think back to my own childhood, growing up in Sunday School, in a church school, which was normal for most children of that time. My parents read me Bible stories, said prayers with me, encouraged me in Sunday School, church organizations, church attendance, as did other parents with their children. We learned the basic facts of the Christian faith, became familiar with the Bible, the Prayer Book, with church life, and this very familiarity provided a firm foundation for life, gave a security, a base which has held firm for life in a changing world. Not all my friends by any means remain members of the Church, but at least they were provided, as I was, with a basis for an informed decision, able to make our own personal choice as we grew older.

I get so frustrated when people say to me today, 'It's up to the children whether they go to church or not. I'm not going to influence them – I was made to go to church when I was a child, and I am not going to force them . . .' My retort is, 'So you leave it to your child to decide whether he cleans his teeth, has a wash, goes to bed, uses a knife or fork, says "thank you" or bothers to turn up at school?' They tell me that is a different matter altogether – I think not! Sadly today we are now into a third generation of 'make your own mind up later' and the result is not of people being able to make an informed decision, but of ignorance and apathy. They may know every 'soap opera' plot, be able to operate the latest technological wonder, and recite the life history of the erring 'royal' or current chart toppers, but how to order their own lives, live in society, cope with matters of life and death and find a purpose and strength to enable them to fulfil their inner longings and hopes is beyond them.

Clifford Longley, writing in *The Daily Telegraph* recently said this: 'Only when people are treated like spiritual beings will they begin to feel like spiritual beings, and come to understand again what being made in the image of God really means. We used to know.' How true that is, but I see signs of hope as I go into schools, as I see and talk with the children in our Church, and with those like my young friends who were not afraid to knock on my door and ask questions 'because we want to know'. All they need is a helping hand, a listening ear, and loving guidance. Surely that is not too much for them to expect, or for us to give?

> Teach children how they should live, and they will remember it all their lives. (Proverbs 22.6 GNB adapted)

> But as for you, continue in the truths that you were taught and firmly believe. You know who your teachers were, and you remember that ever since you were a child, you have known the Holy Scriptures, which are able to give you the wisdom that leads to salvation through faith in Christ Jesus. (2 Timothy 3.14–15 GNB)

Thank you, Father, for faithful and loving parents, teachers and friends, who helped me to grow up to know and love you. Help me to share the riches of your word, the good news of Jesus and the experiences of faith with the children I meet day by day.

SURPLUS TO
REQUIREMENTS

I was surprised to see him turn up at our house on a Thursday morning – usually he was at work this time of day. He didn't look as though he was on holiday: no jaunty step, no casual clothes, just normal – but different. He came in and sat down heavily, and without looking up said 'I was made redundant yesterday.' What do you say? I said 'Do you want a coffee?' He said he did, more to break the feeling of shock which had suddenly wrapped us round like an icy wind. Then, his words tumbling out, he told us his story, of going in to work, being called in to the office and the news being broken to him that he was being made redundant, that they were very sorry but . . . and of course they would help him all they could . . . and if he wanted to leave straight away they would understand . . . He turned the coffee mug round in his hands, and looked into it, as though looking for guidance. 'Twenty-three years I've been there, I'm forty-one next month, what do I do?' The coffee or the company, or the combination of both, seemed to help him to relax a little. After all, it wasn't easy coming to tell your friends you have been made redundant – 'superfluous', as the dictionary puts it. Whatever way you look at it, it means you are not needed, not wanted, not part of the plan for the future. We felt so sad for him, and for his wife. He was what I call 'the old style company man'. Third generation to work for that particular local concern, always so proud of his firm, their achievements, of his own part in it all. Whatever was asked of him, he gave in full measure, because he enjoyed his work, even when it meant doing extra, working 'unsocial hours'. He considered it a duty and a pleasure to do so. Work was his major preoccupation, but looking to the future he had thought about taking 'early retirement' in another ten years or so, ease up, have more time for his home, his hobbies, and they would be financially secure by then . . . he would decide when the time came, but now the decision had been made suddenly and far too early for him. He was joining the vast army of the redundant, the unemployed.

We sat and listened, and talked. It was so much like a bereavement visit, going over the past, the 'what ifs'. The same sort of expression on his face that I see on the face of the newly bereaved – in shock, unable to take in the implications. Sudden death, 'the chop' the numbness, the pain, anger, fear, then grabbing at some signs of hope like a drowning man holding on to a flimsy piece of wreckage in a wild sea. Trying to 'come to terms', as they put it, with something so new, so awful, and so personal. Trying to salvage a little hope, and project it into an uncertain future.

It is early days for him, but he has already begun to take up the possible options, one of which is to go back into full-time education, get some qualifications, make some sort of sense out of what has happened, and try and use it as best he can. He is taking a philosophical attitude towards his situation. 'Well, I suppose I was in a rut there, it was maybe a way of getting me out of it.' But he knows, as we know, that he enjoyed his work, he was happy there, rut or no rut, and now he is faced with all sorts of dilemmas he had never thought about before. He will be yet another dot in the statistics, those figures politicians shuffle around to prove their points, for as they say, 'you can prove anything by statistics', but it is not much fun when you are part of them, on the line that says 'unemployed'.

Our friend has joined the ranks of millions, the unemployed, the redundant, 'out of work'. Their ranks include former high-salaried, highly qualified executives and the 'semi-skilled and unskilled' workers. Those who have never worked, teenagers, bored to death, some driven to crime – stealing cars and mugging old ladies. The good tradesmen, proud craftsmen, are now finding their long apprenticeships and excellent records count for nothing when you are in your forties or fifties and your firm has either closed down or rationalized – a fancy word for cutting back to the bone. There was a time, a few years ago, when we in the north alone suffered from the acute problems of unemployment and redundancies, when north of Watford was a closed book to the so-called affluent south. The challenge was issued: 'Get on your bikes' – a challenge born of ignorance of the position of the people that challenge was addressed to. 'On your bikes' has a hollow ring now when the south has come to experience what we in the north had long suffered from; whether you live north or south of Watford, the tentacles of unemployment and redundancy reach out in all directions.

Only those who have been made redundant, their families and friends, can really appreciate the effect it has on a person: how demoralized they feel, the loss of dignity, the sense of being thrown on a scrap heap, and with no future. Financial problems are not the only ones which afflict them. Mental and physical problems, domestic upheaval, the breakdown of family and personal relationships, guilt, apathy, misery, loss of confidence, of hope for the future.

There are of course the success stories, those who have overcome such a blow and climbed back. There are first-class retraining schemes, opportunities for a new life, but such a drop in the ocean in the sea of unemployment. The gap widens between the 'haves' and 'have nots' – those who have work and those who do not. There is also a growing spirit of moral blackmail amongst some employers, taking advantage of the situation: 'If you don't like it, you know what you can do.' Men and women look over their shoulder at their workmates, seeing them as competitors rather than colleagues.

The Church, through its leaders, national organizations and in its work of industrial mission is in the forefront of pressing for action, for help for the unemployed. On public platforms and from the pulpits they have taken up the cause of the unemployed, and are often criticized for it as being 'left-wing'. The work that is being done through the Church by Christians is so often unnoticed, unpublicized, yet it goes on, in the name of Christ who gave all men and women a dignity, whatever their position. What can individuals do, though? Jesus spoke about the value of those who gave a cup of cold water in his name to those in need. For 'cold water' read tea or coffee, and sympathy, friendship, encouragement, support. Men and women are made in the image of God, and Jesus came 'that you might have life, life in all its fullness', and a full life surely means one in which you can work, provide, learn, share, and have a dignity, a place in society through your own contribution as a person. We all have something to give to the whole, whether it is through paid employment, voluntary work, sharing our skills and knowledge, being appreciated for who and what we are, regardless of status in the world's eye. We need to affirm one another as people, precious, special, wanted, valued. When the ground is knocked from beneath someone's feet we can hold them firm, set them alongside us, and so enable them to stand upright and confident again, our brothers and sisters, together, part of God's family here on earth.

If you put an end to oppression, to every gesture of contempt, and to every evil word; if you give food to the hungry and satisfy those who are in need, then the darkness around you will turn to the brightness of noon. (Isaiah 58.9b—10)

Lord,
we pray for those without work; those who have never had a job, those who have been made redundant, and those who are in fear of losing the job they have. Help us to support them with our love, our prayers, our time and genuine concern, that they may know they are valued for themselves, that they matter to us and to you, and so find in their darkness of despair, light and hope.

THANK YOU FOR
THE DAYS

It was just one of those very happy occasions that live
on in my mind, and will continue to do so for a very
long time. Maybe because I had not expected it to be
quite like that. After all, all the people involved were
going through a tough time, a day in, day out struggle.
For some it had been a lifetime of difficulty, for others
it had gradually come upon them, and for quite a
number, suddenly, like a bolt out of the blue, their
lives had been turned upside down; and for all of
them it meant restrictions, frustrations, unending demands, and a very large question mark over their own
future, and that of their loved ones. Yet looking at
them, seeing the smiles on their cheerful faces, listening to that happy buzz of conversation, it was evident
that they were confident, secure and deeply committed to the task of overcoming barriers, and in spite
of their own problems, to supporting one another, encouraging one another, reaching out with compassion,
humour and understanding.

The occasion was the annual Carers' Service, being
held in Selby Abbey, and the people there were both
carers and those they cared for, of all ages, with varying
degrees of disabilities. There were also family and
friends, members of various organizations, representa-
tives from the local community and civic leaders, all
coming together to share in praise to God, to pray for
one another, and to seek for strength and encouragement in their own situation. The highlight for me that

afternoon was a song sung by members of a group called Fast Track; they belonged to a Day Centre in town and had put in enormous effort to get that item just right. They had rehearsed both at the Centre and in the Abbey, encouraged by their young conductor, and now on THE day came forward proudly and confidently to sing. Only a small group, but what they lacked in numbers they made up for by sheer exhilaration, enjoying to the full making music, the words of the song coming over with such joy and confidence, expressing how they felt about life, what life meant to them. 'Thank you for the days' . . . a song of genuine thankfulness. It touched every heart and the applause rang round and round those ancient Abbey walls, echoing back our grateful thanks to them for reminding us of the joy of each day, whatever the circumstances.

Often as I go to visit someone who is having to cope with enormous problems, suffering or disability, I wonder what on earth I am going to say, and yet find time and time again they minister to me, by their sheer courage and faith, patience and humour. I think of Muriel, 90 now, unable to move even a finger, confined to a chair in a nursing home. Once the life and soul of the church and of the Mothers Union, she still is as active through prayer and interest as the fittest and most able member. She is still valued and much loved. Thank God for her, and all she contributes by being her. She may not be able to move her body, but she can talk, laugh, pray, listen, her eyes twinkle and her smile makes the dullest day light up. If I attempt to sympathize she just smiles at me and says, 'Oh, there's plenty a lot worse off than me' – and yes, she is right, for she has that indomitable spirit that comes from her faith and trust in God, her love of people, and her ability to rise above the paralysis which confines her body but not her spirit.

There are times when my desk is sinking under a pile of things to be done, letters to be answered, deadlines to meet, and I wonder whether it is all worth while, and then the post will arrive and there will be just the encouragement I need from someone I have never even met, like Ted from Guernsey who wrote to thank me for something I had written:

> . . . the verse on page fourteen 'How good is the God we adore' really came to me, you see I am now seventy-seven and lately after many years I have had to give in and stop playing with the Army Band in the open air services. I have also found that I cannot sing as I used to, but the Lord has found me something new to do. On Friday mornings I stand in our Market Place selling 'The War Cry' which also means meeting old friends and chaps I went to school with, so I pray I can carry on doing this. That new book of yours was a real help to me, I often use your books in my quiet time . . .

Thank God for Fast Track, for the Muriels and Teds of this life who by their joy in the Lord, their love and grit and sheer thankfulness lift others up, give them just the boost they need. They refresh the parts that even the most eloquent sermon, the most scholarly paper, could never touch. They are spiritual 'jump leads' to revive and set into motion again those, like me, who sometimes find our batteries of life are very flat indeed! Thank YOU for the days, the hours, the moments you freely give to us, who sometimes find our handicaps hold us down, our shortcomings imprison us, until we are released by your love.

Your life in Christ makes you strong, and his love comforts you. You have fellowship with the Spirit,

and you have kindness and compassion for one
another. (Philippians 2.1–2 GNB)

> Eternal God and Father,
> you create us by your power,
> and redeem us by your love.
> Guide and strengthen us by your Spirit,
> that we may give ourselves in love and service
> to one another and to you,
> through Jesus Christ our Lord. Amen.
> (Collect from *The Alternative Service Book 1980*,
> copyright © The Central Board of Finance of
> the Church of England)

THE LANGUAGE OF
HEAVEN

Why I still do it at my age I do not know, but one of the first columns I turn to in any newspaper, be it local, national or church, is the 'Situations Vacant' column. Letting my imagination run riot, I decide how I would cope with this job or that, how I would deal with the situation described. As a former Personnel Officer I am fascinated by the wording of employment advertisements, as I acquired a certain skill at reading between the lines and, in the jargon of today, at recognizing the hidden agenda.

A recent advertisement in the church press asked for someone with 'initiative, pastoral gift, Bible teaching, group skills and a sense of fun'. I most certainly had a pleasant few minutes thinking about the scope of that one! Of course it was that 'sense of fun' bit that appealed to me, for surely it is one of the most important qualities needed in today's world, and sadly missing in so many people. A recent survey pronounced that 'British people are filled with unprecedented gloom about virtually every aspect of life', and while I recognize that life is a serious matter I still hold to the view that a sense of fun, the ability to laugh, is a Godsend. It is also health-giving, according to some recent research by the American Association for Therapeutic Humour, who found that 'laughter causes healthy physical changes in the body, for it relaxes the body by reducing blood pressure, deepens breathing and improves the circulation – like exercise, only more enjoyable'. Whether that is true or not I leave to you to decide, but I do find a sense of fun, being able to laugh at yourself, and with others, does help defuse difficult situations and gets things into a better perspective. As I read the account of creation it seems to have so much joy and excitement about it. God enjoying creating his world, bringing it to birth, delighting in it, and St Paul, who does not always seem the most humorous of men, writing to his young friend Timothy speaks of God as the one 'who generously gives us everything for our enjoyment'. God wants us to enjoy life – we often forget that. A poster advertising a youth event in our church read 'Putting the forgotten factor back into faith – fun!' I liked that, and hoped not only the youth but all of us would get the message.

A definition of humour I once read said 'genuine humour is always kindly and gracious. It points out the weakness of humanity, but shows no contempt and leaves no sting.' Some of our so-called comedians would do well to heed that. I find children a perpetual source of fun, with their delight in life, in their discovering of new things, and of course the fact they say what they think and tell you how they feel. No wonder Jesus said that unless we become as little children we will not see the kingdom of heaven, for heaven is full of fun and laughter, I am sure of that, and if we have no sense of fun what would we be doing there?

A sense of humour is not confined to the young though. Often I find those who are old in years, perhaps having to bear a great deal of suffering, restriction and sadness, have the most marvellous sense of humour, and are the givers of joy to all they meet. I think of Gwen, a bundle of fun and energy, a quick wit with an impish sense of humour. She belonged to a House Group I led, and her comments and asides were the highlights of our meetings. Then sadly she had a stroke which took her speech. She was so frustrated, became so sad. She lost her sense of fun, because she could no longer express it. It was a tragedy for her and for all of us. We prayed she would regain that wonderful gift, and when she was very ill, on the eve of her ninety-third birthday I went to see her. As I sat beside her she opened her eyes, and they twinkled as they did years ago, her face lit in an enormous smile, and she was able to speak, which I found quite staggering. I had taken her a card and she insisted on opening it there and then. Holding it in both hands she laughed and laughed. She was the old Gwen again, and her frail body shook with delight. As I laid hands on her I thanked God for healing her, giving her back her laughter, her joy, her sense of fun. Not one foot in the grave, but one foot in heaven – she was on her way, and the party had already begun. I remember an elderly priest telling me some years ago that he believed laughter was the language of heaven. I am sure it is too, for I heard it and shared in it at the bedside of an elderly saint of God.

> Sing for joy to the Lord, all the earth;
> > praise him with songs and shouts of joy!
> Sing praises to the Lord!
> > play music on the harps!
> Blow trumpets and horns,
> > and shout for joy to the Lord, our King.
> (Psalm 98.4–6 GNB)

Humour is the prelude to faith, and laughter is the beginning of prayer. (Reinhold Niebuhr)

Peace starts with a smile. (Mother Teresa)

Father,
thank you for shared fun, laughter, humour, that can lift us up even when things are hard. Thank you for those who make us laugh, whose warm and friendly smiles cheer our hearts and lives. May your joy and your peace fill each moment of our lives, and overflow into the lives of all we meet, so together we may praise you for your loving kindness, and rejoice in your salvation. Amen, Praise the Lord!

A RECIPE FOR LIVING

The legend of the Yorkshire pudding has many versions, but the one I enjoy most tells of a weary, hungry traveller arriving at the door of a remote Yorkshire farmhouse. He knocks and asks the good lady for help; she is a kindly soul and welcomes him in, sits him down by the fire, and invites him to help himself to the food on the table. He is so hungry, he polishes the lot off, apart from a bit of dripping in the bottom of the dish. The anxious lady exclaims 'My husband will be home in a few minutes – what can I give him for his dinner? There is nothing left for him.' The traveller says 'Do not fear, put the dish in the oven, get it so hot it smokes. Now have you some flour, a pinch of salt, an egg, and some milk?' The ingredients are brought, the traveller – who is an angel in disguise – beats them together with the tip of his wing, and pours the mixture into the smoking dish, before he disappears, back into heaven. The farmer comes in, sniffing the air appreciatively. 'Something smells good,' he says, as he sits down at the table. His wife opens the oven, and there it is, risen up in the dish, golden brown, crispy and curling. The farmer tucks in. It is so light, yet so satisfying, and the flavour . . . 'This is the best dinner you've ever made, what is it?' His wife smiles, 'Just Yorkshire pudding, luv, just Yorkshire pudding!'

Well, whatever you make of that, or any of the other tales concerning Yorkshire puddings, it is true they are the pride of Yorkshire, although today you will find them in the strangest places throughout the land, and even overseas, and served with every sort of sweet or savoury accompaniment. But the best are still those made in Yorkshire. To my surprise a while ago I saw 'frozen Yorkshire puddings' on sale in the supermarkets. 'Who would buy frozen Yorkshire puddings?' I asked myself, feeling it was an insult to all Yorkshire-pudding makers, but the time came when I decided to try these frozen substitutes for the real thing, and discovered they were just as good, if not better than mine – but then I have only been in Yorkshire since 1970 so have not yet perfected the art of the Yorkshire pudding. So easy are they to cook and serve I did not even need to read the packet, just put them into the oven, until the day I tipped some out of their containers into the hot fat, quite confident of the result. To my horror I opened the oven door to see a sliding mess of batter, which turned into a thin cardboardy substance, more suitable for mending shoes than serving up with roast beef. The trouble was I had picked up a different variety from the supermarket, which were not the ready cooked, but the ready frozen – quite a different matter – and when I retrieved the discarded, the unread packet, I found the instructions read: 'Do not take out of foil containers until cooked', proving I can fail in the most simple of tasks through not paying attention to the details on the packet. It has taught me now to read instructions carefully, and follow them, even when I am quite sure I know everything there is to know about the product.

Listening to a safety expert speaking the other day on the radio I was interested to hear him say that he reckoned over 90 per cent of people never read the instructions on appliances, or when assembling kits. 'They all think they know how, that's how they get in such a mess with them.' I nodded in agreement, re-membering not only those Yorkshire puddings but many other things I have come to grief over. Not just things either, but people, relationships. Rushing in without 'reading the signs', or taking advice. A minute or two of thought, a moment of reflection, would have saved a lot of trouble. It has been said 'fools dash in, where angels fear to tread', and our foolish dashing in without thought can have disastrous results. It is so easy to make instant judgements, rash statements, without thinking. People are delicate, fragile beings, who can be bruised, hurt, even destroyed by clumsy misunderstandings. Once a relationship is broken it can be hard to put it together again. Even the strongest, hardiest, most confident-seeming people have their breaking points. We can never judge by outward appearances, and we do well to bear in mind the warning note that is seen on goods in transit: 'Handle with care'. Every human being is 'in transit', you and I included. If we learn how to handle each other with loving care, sensitivity and understanding, then we will enable one another to fulfil our God-given purpose in life. It all depends on whether we have the sense to follow the maker's instructions, doesn't it?

Trust in the Lord with all your heart.
Never rely on what you think you know.
Remember the Lord in everything you do,
and he will show you the right way.
(Proverbs 3.5–6 GNB)

Lord,
it is so easy to rush into situations, come to conclusions and pass judgement without thinking, without understanding. Remind us of your promise that if we ask, your Holy Spirit will guide us into all truth. Help us to listen before we speak, so that when we speak our words may reflect your wisdom, your truth and your love.

THEN THE SPIRIT CAME

Having sampled all the delights at the centre of the showground, including the heavy horses display, and the Women's Institute tent with all its mouth-watering produce, having visited the show animals and admired the display of vintage vehicles, we began to explore the outskirts and found ourselves following signs marked 'To the hot air balloon'. We discovered a wide stretch of grass with a roped-off arena in the centre of which stood a large basket, looking for all the world like a monster picnic basket, with masses of ropes, various piles of equipment and, in a long straggling heap on the ground, the balloon – although it looked nothing like a balloon, rather more a giant sausage skin. We joined the crowd of people behind the arena and stood watching the frantic toing and froing of three men in overalls. It had just got to the stage when we were losing interest and preparing to walk away and look for something more exciting when we saw that the large mass of balloon was beginning to inflate, so we decided to stay a while longer. As the balloon was inflated we began to see the beautiful design on it filling out. It was truly magnificent. We were then invited to get in to the basket – as so many wanted a turn we decided to remain spectators! In twos and threes people were helped in and out of that giant basket, while one of the organizers came round with cards for us all, telling us how much it would cost for a trip. The conversation around us we found fascinating. 'I tell you, you wouldn't get me going in that thing . . . I don't think it's safe . . . I heard of one crashing . . . Eh, it must be a wonderful feeling . . . I wouldn't pay that, just for a trip in a basket . . . Not with my back I wouldn't . . .' I noticed the balloon was straining to be up, up and away, the huge ropes which tethered it were taut, and then, as the first paying customers climbed in there was a whoosh as the flames went up inside the balloon, the ropes were released and that great mass began to lift off into the sky. We all stood gazing up at that dramatic scene, and soon the balloon was going off over the showground, higher and higher, until it disappeared out of our view.

Later on, I saw a couple who had gone up in the balloon, flushed with excitement, proudly wearing big badges which said 'I've been up in the balloon!' They were busy sharing their story with a little crowd of admirers. I nudged my friend: 'Look, there's some good free advertising going on, they will sell more trips than all of those cards. One of these days I may well take a trip myself!'

Thinking about it afterwards I couldn't help but compare that experience at the show to the life of the Church. So often all that is to be seen is a lot of people running around a pile of lifeless tackle and nothing happening, so those outside the Church cannot see any point in belonging to such an ineffectual group. Then maybe, just maybe, something stirs, there are some signs of life. Outsiders can see possibilities, and so with a bit of encouragement are willing to try it for size, get into the basket you might say – or into the pew or seat – but still nothing really happens, so they get out, and go away. But sometimes, yes, just some-times it happens, it all makes sense, and there is 'lift off', there is life and power and freedom, and being part of it transforms them, and they can't wait to share their experience with everyone they meet, and how proudly they wear their badge of allegiance to Christ now! To the doubter, waverers, cynics, fearful, they can give their own personal testimony, 'We know, it's true!'

What the Church today stands in need of is the whoosh, the power, to have the courage to let go of the heavy restricting ropes that keep it earthbound, so that it can be what it was intended to be, and those who experience it, who know it, can share it, can be walking, talking, living witnesses. The glorious truth is that the power is here already, the Holy Spirit has come, is alive and active, if only we will realize it and allow ourselves to be taken by the Holy Spirit to fulfil our purpose, our mission.

On Ascension Day Jesus was taken up into heaven. His friends could only gaze open-mouthed, almost rooted to the ground, but the angels had firm words for them: 'Why are you standing there looking up at the sky? This Jesus, who was taken from you into heaven, will come back in the same way that you saw him go into heaven' (Acts 1.11 GNB). So they began to get on with the job, getting the tackle sorted you may say, doing what they could do, filling the gaps, and all the time looking forward for the promised Holy Spirit to come and empower them . . . and he did! On the day of Pentecost, the Spirit came! Awesome, terrifying, powerful, in wind, fire, sight and sound, filling the followers of the Risen, Ascended Lord with power, more dramatic than any take off of a hot air balloon or supersonic flight. Filled with the Holy Spirit they could now accomplish great things for the glory of God and the coming of the kingdom, drawing others into the same experience through their testimony of word and life, freed to serve the Lord in the power of the Spirit. This challenges me to ask of myself and to put to you the questions 'Am I still running around a pile of lifeless tackle, or content to stand in a tethered demonstration model? Or am I adventurous enough, obedient enough, to let go of the ropes and allow the Holy Spirit to take me where he wills and to whom he wills?' Three alternatives there – which will it be?

When the day of Pentecost came, all the believers were gathered together in one place. Suddenly there was a noise from the sky which sounded like a strong wind blowing, and it filled the whole house where they were sitting. Then they saw what looked like tongues of fire which spread out and touched each person there. They were all filled with the Holy Spirit, and began to talk in other languages, as the Spirit enabled them to speak. (Acts 2.1–4 GNB)

O breath of life, come sweeping through us,
Revive your Church with life and power,
O breath of life, come cleanse, renew us,
And fit your Church to meet this hour.
(Bessie Porter Head)

Come Holy Spirit, come!

IT'S HEAVEN BY RAIL!

No gleaming high-tech Eurostar or romantic Orient Express, but a plain everyday train, almost hidden away, at the far right-hand side of Leeds Station. No famous name plate, or boasting the latest in passenger amenities, just a mechanical workhorse, part of Regional Railways stock, destined to spend its life chugging up and down a section of northern England. Rather like the people who travelled on it, who were friendly looking, unassuming, some going off to work or to visit friends or relatives, others 'having a day out'. There were men and women with cases, mums with pushchairs, holding on to babies and toddlers, young folk with rucksacks, older ones in walking gear, or set for a day in the country, prepared with their umbrellas, packed lunches and thermos flasks, some with walking sticks, and one or two being helped up on to the train, finding the step as much of a challenge as later on some of those walkers would find the distant hills. Half a dozen trips up to Carlisle in Cumbria, half a dozen trips back from Carlisle to Leeds, in West Yorkshire – such trains would make the journey each day, and who could imagine, looking at that particular train, that it was the vehicle to convey people on one of the most famous and beautiful routes in the whole world, and many would say, THE most famous and most beautiful, the Leeds–Settle–Carlisle line, and at a fraction of the cost of a trip on Eurostar or the Orient Express!

When I had been invited to speak at a conference in Carlisle I had accepted with great pleasure, and not just because of the Conference – in fact my delight had been more to do with the prospect of the journey! What awaited me the other end I was prepared to take in faith – it was the route that held the great attraction.

So it was in a cheerful frame of mind I joined the rest of the passengers that bright sunny morning, and soon we were edging out of the city, leaving behind the high-rise offices and dwellings, the industry, and the drabness of urban sprawl, and moving into the countryside. In a very short time only the odd farms and little groups of houses were to be seen dotted on the horizon, and we were into the Yorkshire Dales. We stopped at neat, well-ordered little railway stations, their names proudly surrounded by flowers, or whitewashed stones, inviting us to step out and sample their welcome, to come and explore what lay beyond.

At each station some passengers alighted, others joined, in ones and twos and threes, a constantly changing variety of people, a constantly changing variety of scenery. On we went, past field after field of sheep with their lambs. The lambs looked inquisitively at us, before dashing off, little tails flying, to the safety of their mothers, who plodded on grazing, for they had seen it all before. Cows lazily raised their heads, and rabbits sitting beside the track gazed bright-eyed with twitching noses at this strange creature without legs rushing by. The green banks splashed yellow with masses of primroses on either side, later giving way to clumps of cowslips. We climbed higher and higher. Now the trees had almost disappeared, and we were high above the landscape, almost into the sky, crossing the Ribbleshead Viaduct. Then through the dark tunnels, the wind whistling through the open windows in the carriages, so much so that the walkers pulled up their anorak hoods, while a stout red-faced gentleman got up and slammed the windows shut with his walking stick. Out again into the light, down came the hoods, the windows were opened again, and the air was fresh and clean and good.

We drew into Dent, 1,150 feet above sea level, then through Garsdale, Kirkby Stephen, into Appleby with its memorial to a former Bishop of Wakefield, Dr Eric Treacy, who died on the station platform back in 1978, a man who was a great railways photographer, who loved railways and railwaymen, 'a lover of life' and a much beloved friend and bishop. The Pennine Moors were now rapidly turning into the lush and fertile Eden Valley, while ahead lay the mountains, the tops still snow-covered, even in May. Then we came clattering into Carlisle Station with an almost jaunty air. We all began to gather up our bags and coats, and as I made my way along the platform I saw a man holding up a large card with the words 'Christian Media 96'. He smiled as he saw me approaching him, held out his hand and said, 'You're Margaret, welcome!' We walked out of the station together, already feeling like old friends. One part of the journey was now behind me, I was ready for the next stage, and for whatever it held.

Life itself is often described as a journey, although it may not always be as pleasant and comfortable as the one I made that bright sunny day in May. Sometimes it is more like a bleak winter's 'stop-start' journey, with frequent delays due to frozen points, reluctant engines and 'unforeseen circumstances', and we sit and fume and wish we had never ventured out, and all we can do is sit and wait and hope for the best. Even on such a journey though it can be brightened by fellow-passengers; maybe it's the British character, but adverse conditions seem to bring out the best in people, a spirit of 'in it together', the flashes of humour, people opening up to one another, 'the Dunkirk spirit'. The passing scenery, fellow-passengers, a good book, and the refreshments available combine to make travelling a pleasure, and the moment of arrival, being welcomed, makes it all worth while. But the greatest pleasure of all is the journey home, that moment when we come home. The journey, whatever it's been like, is done, all that has gone on, success or failure, good or ill, is behind us now we are home, where we belong. One day we will all finish our earthly journey, the travelling will be behind us, we will arrive home, and the Lord will be there to meet us, to welcome us. What a moment that will be! In the meanwhile, we travel on. Let's make the most of our journey, and above all, make sure we are going in the right direction!

> I heard the voice of Jesus say,
> 'I am this dark world's light;
> Look unto me, thy morn shall rise,
> And all thy day be bright':
> I looked to Jesus, and I found
> In him my star, my sun;
> And in that light of life I'll walk,
> Till travelling days are done.
> (Horatius Bonar, 1808–1889)

Father,
as I travel through the world each day,
may I travel hopefully,
cheerfully,
thankfully,
grateful for all your mercies.
Thank you for those who share my journey,
family, friends, strangers,
and above all,
thank you that as you were there at the beginning,
you will be there at the end,
to welcome me home. Amen.

JUST A MINUTE

I'm warm, comfortable, and in the land of sweet dreams – and then the alarm goes, its shrill sound galvanizing me into action so as to stop it before it wakes not only Peter blissfully asleep beside me, but the whole neighbourhood. With a leap, or to be more accurate a shuffle, I get out of bed, while Peter murmurs 'Good, you are up, hope it goes well, see you later' as I quietly leave the bedroom, gathering up my clothes and heading for the bathroom. I look at my watch, it is 5.15 a.m. By 5.30 I am in my car, heading out through the village towards York, 20 miles away. No one about this time of the morning, just an odd car or lorry, but as I get into the city of York, here and there a few shadowy figures, hunched as they walk along. With the Minster in front of me, its huge solid form rather reassuring, I turn left into a car park. At least there is no problem about parking this time of the morning. Having secured my car I walk briskly the last few yards to Radio York. In I go, and a mug of coffee is placed into my hands. Thankfully it brings me back to life, before I'm on air with *Daybreak* at 6.35 a.m. One minute or so to share my thoughts, experiences and faith with the listeners, and for those still slumbering in their beds, it will be repeated at the much more civilized (to my mind!) time of 8.35 a.m. The staff at Radio York are certainly wide awake, but then they have been there at least an hour before me, the presenter full of the joys of spring, road reports, news and weather, and his welcoming smile and comments enable me to give of my best – even at this early point of the day. The airway's all mine for a minute – and it's meant working on the material, trimming it, revamping it, sometimes changing it completely, before I got it to my satisfaction. It has meant getting up early, driving to the studio, and all for a minute – though don't forget the repeat – that's two minutes of air time. Is it worth it? Of course it is.

My week 'on the rota' for BBC Radio Humberside's *Pause for Thought*, which comes round every few months, is a little later, and for a little longer. Going out 'live' around 7.45 a.m. means I can leave home just about 7 o'clock, in time to get to the Goole studio, that rather grand-sounding name for what is actually about the size of a large cupboard on the side of the Goole Library, across from the Police Station, where I have to collect the key to the studio, to enable me to get myself on air. No welcoming faces in this studio, no cup of coffee either, just a bare small room, with all the necessary equipment to connect me to the main studios in Hull. As I put on the headphones, adjust the controls and dial the studio I am welcomed by a cheery voice the other end, who connects me up to the breakfast programme, and leaves me with the promise 'I'll be back' – and sure enough, he is, in time to announce 'and here in our Goole studio, and for all this week, is the Reverend Margaret Cundiff . . . good morning, Margaret . . .' So here I go again, trying to be topical, practical, hard-hitting, amusing, thoughtful, theological and . . . myself! Being the 'Godslot' in a day when for most people maybe God seems to be absent, irrelevant or unapproachable, it's my job to somehow let them know that God loves them, he cares, he is at work in the world and that although Margaret Cundiff does not know all – or many – of the answers to the big questions of life, she knows someone who does, someone who is her friend, and she wants to introduce him to them. I am not a 'hard sell' merchant because I don't believe God is a commodity to be sold, but I can share my experiences of him. Jesus told stories to people who asked questions and left them to decide for themselves, and he used ordinary everyday situations they could relate to. I see myself very much as a story-teller, a story-sharer, and then it's up to the listeners to draw their own conclusions.

Being on *Pause for Thought* on Radio 2 regularly gives me the chance to communicate with a much larger audience but in the same vein, though here I have the luxury of pre-recording, and having three minutes for each slot, also repeated – six minutes of Radio 2, that's quite something. Also I can travel with ease to Manchester by Trans-Pennine Express train to Broadcasting House where I marvel at the scale of everything, and feel very pampered by all the personal attention my producer Claire and all those involved give me. The reason my slots are pre-recorded is that they go out at 1.30 a.m. and 3.30 a.m. When I was first asked to do these slots, many years ago, I laughed and said 'Who on earth listens then?' which was a very silly question, because so many people listen then, and a very sensitive audience too. Just think of all the people who are working, travelling, can't sleep, are worried, anxious, just need to hear a friendly voice, some reassurance, to be brought close to God, to be made to smile, find hope and feel someone understands them. That middle of the night *Pause for Thought* can and does make such a difference to so many people, and I know that by the appreciative letters I receive. Our bodies, and often our spirits, are at their lowest ebb in the middle of the night. Who can help, who can we turn to? The radio is a gift, a lifeline, a personal presence, and to be able to be part of that is an enormous privilege and responsibility.

I am very much a radio person, for it is a very personal medium, a 'one to one'. For well over 20 years I have been going out 'on air' on all sorts of radio programmes, and with all of them I have been enabled to use those opportunities to the full by dedicated and professional staff who make sure I am as effective as possible by their technical skills, advice, encouragement and criticism and above all, their friendship, welcoming smiles, words and those mugs of coffee. Thank God for radio, and all who are involved in it, the voices we hear and the people behind the voices, those we never hear, but without whom our lives would be so much poorer – our understanding of the world beyond our door so limited, and our circle of friends so much smaller. God bless our airwaves and all who serve in them!

What a joy it is to find just the right word for the right occasion! (Proverbs 15.23 GNB)

The Sovereign Lord has taught me what to say, so that I can strengthen the weary. (Isaiah 50.4 GNB)

Father,
we pray for all those who as broadcasters have the opportunity to speak to so many, to influence thought and action. Help them to exercise the gift of speech with integrity, truth and clarity, that the words they speak may enhance the lives of those who listen. We ask it in the name of your Son Jesus Christ, who is the living word.

THERE IS A WORD
FOR IT

The family on the next table to us in the restaurant were just finishing their meal as we sat down to begin ours. They had got to the coffee stage, and the two children with them were looking rather bored, and beginning to get restless as children do. The grandfather, who looked as though he was well used to organizing, said brightly 'Let's play a game. I say a word and you follow on with another one that describes it, and we go round.' This proved a great success, to the point I was almost joining in the fun, but by now I was getting one of those looks from my daughter, Alison, which warned 'Don't listen in to other people's conversation, mother!' So obediently I concentrated on the food on my plate, though, I have to admit, with one ear still on the family game, and the wonderful connections that were being made with words.

Then one of the children said loudly 'daddy' to which the other one replied without a moment's hesitation 'stress'. There was a silence, a shuffling of cups, and shortly after the family got up, paid the bill and left abruptly. I noticed how strained the adults looked, and realized that the word 'stress' had touched a nerve. I also realised that 'daddy', whoever he was, was not with them, for the party consisted of an older man and woman, obviously grandparents, a young woman whom I took to be mother, and the two girls, aged around eight and ten. It was obvious by the adults' faces that 'daddy' and 'stress' did go together, but it was no game, it was for real.

'Stress' – a state many of us find ourselves in, to some degree or other, in the frenetic pace of modern life. All the uncertainties, worries about the environment, pollution, 'mad cow disease' and other ills. Work and family pressures, noise, bills, pains, the sheer pressure of 'keeping up'. We are all affected in some way, part of the price for living at the tail end of the twentieth century. No wonder some people crack up – it all gets just too much for them, and they snap under the burden of it all. It is the 'busy, busy, busy' ever tightening of the springs which suddenly go 'twang' – they cannot take any more. David Adam, in his book *Tides and Seasons*, writes this: '. . . there are lives that let so much flow in that they are unable to accept anything new, people who are always too busy and have no time. There is a great danger of justifying our lives by hyperactivity, or by how much we have amassed.'

Maybe our biggest problem, and I speak for myself too, for I am equally guilty of the busy syndrome, is that we try and project into the future too much, 'tomorrow, next week, next year . . .' We fall over ourselves in trying to get ahead, be ahead, and so load ourselves with impossible burdens, and then spend our time worrying about them. If only we would learn to take life a day at a time we would find it was broken down into quite manageable chunks. That is not to say we should be idle, content to rock gently in our designer safety net, unwilling to take risks and live dangerously at times. A certain amount of stress is good for us, when we are stretched to do something we thought was beyond us, expand our horizons, see a job through and meet those deadlines, even though it means giving ourselves an extra push. But there have to be the slack times too of relaxation, letting go gently before taking the strain again. The old saying 'All work and no play makes Jack a dull boy' – and a poorly boy too – goes for girls as well, of all ages. Watch a 'tug of war' contest, those teams that train to achieve a perfect balance of 'heave and rest, heave and rest'. The control of tension comes from mind and body being in tune, the assurance that all is under control, all is well.

John Greenleaf Whittier expressed this in his hymn 'Dear Lord and Father of Mankind' and especially in the verse which goes,

> Drop thy still dews of quietness,
> Till all our strivings cease;
> Take from our souls the strain and stress,
> And let our ordered lives confess
> The beauty of thy peace.
> (John Greenleaf Whittier, 1807–1892,
> 'Dear Lord and Father of mankind')

It is a matter of simple trust, trust in the Lord to provide all we need, and having done our best to leave it there.

As I lay my head on the pillow each night, whatever sort of a day it has been, I use the prayer Jesus used: 'Father, into your hands I place my spirit' – and then I leave it to him. And tomorrow? Well, that is another day, and as God is there already, it is in good hands, and so am I.

> Jesus said, 'So do not start worrying: 'Where will my food come from? or my drink? or my clothes?' (These are the things the pagans are always concerned about.) Your Father in heaven knows that you need all these things. Instead, be concerned

above everything else with the Kingdom of God, and with what he requires of you, and he will provide you with all these other things. So do not worry about tomorrow; it will have enough worries of its own. There is no need to add to the troubles each day brings.' (Matthew 6.31–34 GNB)

Father,
I worry about so many things, I feel sometimes I have all the world on my shoulders; no wonder I get stressed, anxious, tired. Yet I know you are capable of running the world, my bit of the world – after all, you made it, and me! Teach me to relax in your love and care, to trust you for the mountains and the molehills, allow you to take the strain, and so know the peace of body, mind and spirit which is your gift to me – through Christ Jesus.

'NO PLACE TO GO'

'This is the life' I thought as I parked myself down on a bench looking out at the bluest of blue seas, the tiny fishing boats bobbing up and down in the bay, and the golden sands stretching for miles. 'God's in his heaven, and all's well with the world' – certainly in this part of the world, and if heaven is anything like this, I decided, it will suit me. Filey, on the North Yorkshire coast, is one of my favourite spots for a relaxing day out. Not as busy as Scarborough or Bridlington, not as quaint as Whitby, but with a gentle, rather old-fashioned charm that draws me back over and over again. An easy drive over the Wolds from my home in Selby, a good choice of fish and chip shops, and the delight of sitting in the park overlooking the bay before walking off those fish and chips along the sands. One of those summer days when everything combined to make it a joy just 'to be'. I had a great vantage point as well. I looked across at the lane that straggled down to the beach, enjoying watching the crowd go by. A typical seaside scene, everyone making for the beach. Babies in pushchairs, and being carried. Children chasing along, youngsters holding hands. Mums and dads, grannies and grandpas, folk in wheel-chairs, old folk walking slowly, but all enjoying the glorious day. It was what they were carrying though that caught my attention. Some were staggering along with 'everything but the kitchen sink': towels, brightly coloured buckets and spades, blow-up beds, chairs, mats and windbreaks. Bags of provisions too, lemonade, flasks

69

– well, when you are out for the day you need to be prepared, don't you?

As I looked out at the happy scene, listened to the voices and sounds of people enjoying themselves, being together, I suddenly saw in my mind a similar crowd of people walking along on a sunny day, but in that crowd very few young men, in fact hardly any men at all. On the faces of that crowd walking along together, not eager anticipation of a day at the seaside, or the happy excitement of children, but fear, desperation and grief. Refugees fleeing in Bosnia. Fleeing where? Who knows?

A few possessions, very little, just what they wore, or a bag slung over their shoulder – they couldn't afford to be hindered by luggage, not like us who had all the time in the world, and the prospect of being able to load it up in the car and go home when we were tired. People just like you and me though, just like the happy crowd at Filey that summer's day. People like my family, yours, the folk next door, down the road, but caught up in a dreadful situation which no one seems to be able to do anything about.

'What can I do?' I thought, and I found myself praying as I sat there in Filey, praying for my brothers and sisters in Bosnia, and in those other war-torn parts of the world. Praying for an end to hatred and war, praying for the leaders who make the decisions which affect the lives of so many. Praying for aid organizations, peace-keeping forces, for protection for them, praying that supplies might get through to the right people, and not be misused or diverted to the wrong channels. With my prayer came that nudge which said, 'Well, what are you going to do?' and I realized there was something I could do. I could support those agencies trying to bring aid not just with my prayers but by putting my hand in my pocket, sharing some of my wealth – and it is wealth, compared with so many – to help buy supplies. It may not be a lot, but every little helps, it all counts.

I looked out again at the scene before me, the happiness, the fun, the peace, the sounds of laughter, chatter, people enjoying themselves, and why not? It was time to join them, make my way down to the beach. I looked at my watch – there was the prospect of a couple of relaxing hours before I needed to get back to the car park, drive home, and share my day out with the family. I thanked God not just for my fun and enjoyment and that of those around, but for his reminder of another part of the world. 'God's in his heaven, all's well with the world' – no, God had given me a nudge to remind me he is not just in heaven, but in his world, concerned for it. All is not well, so what am I going to do about it? Later on, as I arrived back home and walked through the door my son smiled at me as he took my bag. 'Had a good day mum?' 'Lovely, thanks' I replied. 'Just in time for the news' said my husband Peter; 'I'll make you a coffee.' The newsreader was just saying '. . . fighting continues in . . .' and there they were, those people, walking along together in a crowd, going nowhere . . . the people I'd seen in my mind's eye that afternoon, but now I was home – where were they?

Rich people who see a brother or sister in need, yet close their hearts against them, cannot claim that they love God. My children, our love should not be just words and talk. It must be true love, which shows itself in action. (1 John 3.17-18 GNB)

Lord,
thank you for all you have given me to enjoy: the beauty and peace of the world around me, the joy of family and friends, the provision for my needs, over and above all I can desire. Keep me mindful of the needs of others, and enable me to do all I can to help, through prayer, concern and practical action, my brothers and sisters whose lives are marred by war and oppression. Give peace in our time, O Lord – and use me, in any way possible, to be an instrument of that peace. Amen.

KEEP COOL

'Come on, move' I muttered to myself through gritted teeth. But there was no chance of moving, the queue of traffic went on as far as the eye could see, which was not surprising – after all, it was Monday, and Monday in Selby means one thing, Market Day. Our town is bursting at the seams on Mondays, and with the volume of traffic it is a real headache trying to get in or out. It wouldn't have been so bad but it was so hot, a scorcher; even with the window open it was like being in an oven, and not helped by the fumes issuing from the car in front. I could see the driver drumming impatiently on his steering wheel as he kept revving his engine. 'It won't make you go any quicker' I thought angrily as I gave my accelerator a quick burst in tune with his. Then from nowhere a car shot past us, ignoring all oncoming traffic, and disappeared off to the right. The whole line of us leaned on our horns and sent a unanimous message of disapproval. The temperature visibly rose, and it wasn't anything to do with the air outside either.

That feeling of annoyance remained with me for quite some time, and I realized I was experiencing the ailment 'road rage'. This has become a very serious problem on our roads today as drivers get angry and aggressive with their fellow drivers. Sadly sometimes it doesn't stop at horn-blowing or muttered words and signals of disapproval, but has led to physical assaults and even murder, often triggered off by some small irritation that blows up like a volcano with disastrous consequences.

Of course it is not just on the roads but in every area of life. Tempers flare, fists fly and things get out of hand. I was listening to a mother screaming at her two children the other day, and the words she was using were beyond coarse and obscene. She was in such a temper she probably didn't realize what she was saying. She was certainly oblivious of those around her, listening to her outburst, or of the effect on her children, both little more than toddlers.

It is said 'crimes of passion' are on the increase, and domestic violence is commonplace. Certainly the world generally has got more violent. 'Shouting matches' are played out in the full glare of publicity. On the sports field, in Parliament, by 'protesters' for every cause under the sun and even in some church affairs. Listening to that mother I wondered, where is self-control these days? . . . and then I remembered my little temper tantrum, my anger, that reflex action which betrayed my lack of control. I felt ashamed of myself, and brought it before God, asking for forgiveness, and strength to resist that urge which is within me to hit out when things don't go my way. A couple of days later I was reading the set lesson for the day; it was from the Sermon on the Mount, and it certainly came home sharply to me that my little temper outburst was just as bad in God's eyes as that of someone who is guilty of 'grievous bodily harm', for it was the same attitude to a fellow human being. I was guilty, and had no excuse. Looking back on it now I am glad I was brought up sharp by the words of Jesus. They came right when I needed to hear them, and so I am doing my best to keep my temper, even when I feel provoked or the innocent party, for provoked I may often be, but innocent party? – I very much doubt it. Losing our tempers over small things often leads to situations getting out of hand. Anger acts like a match to explosives – better to cool it and to seek to practise courtesy and self-control; it is good sense as well as good behaviour, something we all need to remember even in a traffic queue during a heat wave!

> Jesus said, 'You have heard that people were told in the past, 'Do not commit murder; anyone who does will be brought to trial.' But now I tell you: whoever is angry with his brother will be brought to trial, whoever calls his brother 'You good-for-nothing!' will be brought before The Council, and whoever calls his brother a worthless fool will be in danger of going to the fire of hell.' (Matthew 5.21-22 GNB)

Lord,
it is so easy to lose my temper, to allow my selfishness and pride to dictate my behaviour. Forgive me, and help me to realize that courtesy and understanding are signs of strength, not weakness, and enable me, by your grace, to live in peace and harmony with all.

LOOK CAREFULLY, AND SEE

I knew of course they didn't work, couldn't work. After all, I had followed the instructions to the letter, read and re-read them, in case I had missed some vital clue. I even tried putting my glasses on the end of my nose and closing one eye, but still nothing happened, the paper remained a flat mass of squiggles. I would not give up though. I have a nature akin to a terrier with a bone – I will not let go! So I reasoned if it would not work for me it would not work for anyone. It was just a big hoax, a gigantic con-trick.

Then, one evening I tried again, and lo and behold it happened, it worked! I was like a child again, almost sick with excitement, boring everyone around me silly with the account of my great discovery.

It was one of those 3-D images, described in the blurb as 'the amazing optical illusion that will change the way you see the world'. I had seen them from time to time, but taken no interest, not caring one way or the other, but one day the words 'change the way you see the world' sprang out from the page and challenged me, and I was determined to find out for myself. For if it was possible to see the world from a different angle, if there was something I was missing out on, then I wanted to know – and now.

Once I had managed to make the 3-D image come into focus, it was a simple matter to do it again. Now I pick up the paper confidently and stare into the jumble knowing that the picture is there all right, and I will see it. I have proved it so time and time again, it is a secret no longer. Now I look for those pictures, eager to see them, and I find them in all sorts of places. I think I must have been blind not to notice them before. There are even books of them, one of which is near to hand now, ready to be dipped into and enjoyed. They have not changed the way I see the world – that claim was rather extravagant – but they have given me new insight into the way our minds work, and perhaps given me more sympathy towards those who find life rather difficult to sort out. They have to endure others telling them it is a simple matter – 'Just have faith, that's all you need' – when faith is the last thing they find possible in trying to make sense of their situation.

For me, coming to faith was fairly simple I suppose. As a teenager who wanted to know, with an 'all or nothing' attitude to life, once I was challenged to look at Jesus, to be open to him, and to respond, I did it. The flat, uncoordinated view I had of life at that point burst into focus, even more stunningly exciting than the 3-D picture. As for changing the way I saw the world, it most certainly did. What is more, it changed the way I saw God, saw other people, and saw myself. Perhaps the biggest problem, though, was that I expected others to have the same experience as well, and found it very frustrating when they didn't, and couldn't.

Failing to get the 3-D picture immediately 'on demand' has helped me understand how people feel when, although they want to have faith, want to believe, it 'just doesn't happen'. As a friend said to me sadly, 'It's all right for you – you have had an experience of God, I haven't. It may make sense to you, but it doesn't for me – I wish it did.' The old expression 'You can take a horse to the water, but you can't make it drink' is true about the Christian faith. It is no use pushing people, bombarding them with proof texts, thrusting literature into their hands, arguing the point. Jesus never treated people like that; he loved them and respected them too much to do that. He did not force, bully, cajole, but touched them with his love and issued an invitation 'Follow me . . . come and see . . .' When they saw him, what he was, who he was, they wanted to know more. Yet even those closest to him did not realize to the full extent what that entailed – there were still blurs – but what they did see was enough to make them continue in their desire to know, to understand, to be like him. From the everyday experience of being with him on earth, to knowing he was risen from the dead, was for some an instant experience, for others a gradual awareness, for many a long haul, some rejecting him fiercely before coming to the point of seeing him as Saviour, as Lord and as God. It is the same today. Coming to faith is a different path for each one of us, there are as many paths as people, but the promise of Jesus holds true: '. . . you will know the truth and the truth will set you free'.

The compilers of those 3-D pictures know beyond doubt the pictures are there to be discovered – naturally, for they have created the pictures. The instructions are given, the way explained, but it is up to us to decide whether to try, to persevere, to give up or to deny them. That is our privilege, or our loss. God has given us his Son Jesus. God is the author of all life; through Jesus he has given us the opportunity to receive the gift of his new life, and the power of the Holy Spirit to sustain us. He has provided us with instructions, through the Bible, through the example of faithful people, and he gives us the seed of faith, deep within us, which contains the desire, the urge to know, to grow, to see life in a new way. Maybe I am just beginning to learn that to stand back, to pray, just to be there when needed is the greatest aid I can be to others who are struggling 'to get the picture', to discover for themselves the faith to enable them to walk with Jesus along the pathway that leads to life.

The next day John was standing there again with two of his disciples, when he saw Jesus walking by. 'There is the Lamb of God!' he said. The two disciples heard him say this and went with Jesus. Jesus turned, saw them following him, and asked, 'What are you looking for?' They answered, 'Where do you live, Rabbi?' (This word means 'teacher'.) 'Come and see,' he answered. (It was then about four o'clock in the afternoon.) So they went with him, and saw where he lived, and spent the rest of that day with him. (John 1.35–39 GNB)

Lord,
help me not to stand in the way of your invitation to 'come and see', either by the strength or by the weakness of my profession of faith, but to follow humbly and joyfully in your footsteps.

ONLY A PEBBLE

I took my sandals off and walked along the shore, pausing to pick up some shells, admiring their colours and shapes, before putting them into a bag in my pocket. The water was warm and clear, and the waves gently lapping over my feet and legs gave me a feeling of utter bliss and contentment. I made my way along to a secluded area, hidden by rocks, and sat down in the sunshine, gazing out at sea. I could see tiny fishing boats bobbing up and down in the distance; the only sound was of the birds calling to one another and the flip, flop of the water, just a yard or so from me. I scrabbled in the sand with my hand and brought out a pebble, a small, round, very ordinary-looking pebble, and just held it in my hand. It gave me a sense of comfort, security, peace. Such an ordinary pebble – there were millions around, I could have picked up any one, but this was special. Then I felt the tears running down my face. I thought back four years ago, when I had been so excitedly looking forward to a trip to the Holy Land. A 'chance of a lifetime' to spend a few days there. My mother had shared my excitement, wanting to know every last detail of the trip. When I saw her just four days before I was due to fly out she reminded me yet again, 'Now don't go spending your money on me. All I want is a pebble from the Sea of Galilee. I've always wanted one.' Gaily I promised her I would bring back a pebble for her, specially picked. As we waved goodbye to each other that day I had no idea it would be for the last time. Two days later came the phone call. My mother had died suddenly. She did not get her pebble from the Sea of Galilee, neither did I make the journey there; instead it was to her funeral held in the little village church in Cheshire, and later on to her childhood home village of Dunster where we scattered her ashes, the following spring.

Four years later, I had been offered another trip to the Holy Land. It had come quite out of the blue, and so I had jumped at the chance. Now here I was, by the Sea of Galilee. I breathed in that wonderful air, looked out at the scene before me, imagining how Jesus must have often been out on that sea in a boat very much like one of those I could see on the horizon. He too had walked along the seashore, here he had met his friends, shared in meals, encouraged and supported them, and given his friend Peter a new beginning. My hand tightened on the pebble. 'I've got it for you, mum, a bit late, but I've got it.' There were tears of sadness that I couldn't put that pebble in my mother's hand, tears of joy because I knew she had 'entered into the joy of her Lord'. Heaven and earth merged together as I sat there, and it was very reluctantly I tore myself away from that special spot and made my way back slowly along the shore to meet up with the rest of our party.

I often look at that pebble, hold it in my hand, a reminder of a promise made, a promise kept, but more than that, of life being held secure and safe in God's hand, his promise made, his promise kept.

You are all round me on every side, you protect me with your power . . . If I flew away beyond the east or lived in the farthest place in the west, you would be there to lead me, you would be there to help me. (Psalm 139.5, 9–10 GNB)

Father,
thank you that I can trust you with everything and everybody, in life and in death. Thank you for the gift of human love, for all I have enjoyed and will enjoy in the future, above all, for your love which sustains me and holds me safe today and always.

WHATEVER NEXT?

In the space of one day I was asked the same question in a slightly different way by three entirely different people. Taking part in a radio discussion programme I was asked 'Have you made adequate provision for the future?'; by a colleague, 'Where do you see your ministry going in the next five years?'; and by a friend on hearing I had almost finished writing this book, 'So what do you think you will do next?' I was tempted to answer to the first, 'I have my passport for heaven at the ready'; to the second, 'Forward'; and to the third, 'Climb Everest', but decided to be tactful and so made appropriate noises which I hope satisfied all my enquirers. I did throw in to all three though my favourite Woody Allen quotation, 'If you want to make God laugh tell him your future plans', because I have long since discovered that God has a wonderful way of changing my plans completely and replacing them with something infinitely better. Based on experience I know I can trust in his judgement absolutely, as it so wisely says in the Book of Proverbs: 'You may make your plans, but God directs your actions' (Proverbs 16.9 GNB). Yet the questions remain, and are very real and pertinent questions. Whoever we are, we have to make plans for each day, otherwise we would not get through it. Even the simplest tasks require an element of planning, as anyone will realize who has ever run out of milk on a Bank Holiday, or failed to take notice of the petrol gauge on their car before setting out on a journey. We need to make plans personally for the things that affect our lives, but even more so within the wider scheme of life. As members of a family, community, organization, business, church, or whatever, we have our common responsibilities. We need to work together, to plan and carry out those plans for the good of the whole, and that means looking at options, possibilities, coming to decisions and acting accordingly. It requires the delicate art of negotiation, of being sensitive to the needs of others, aware of their strength and weaknesses, being able to argue our case firmly, and yet having the good grace to know when to pull back or equally when to push forward, with integrity.

God intends us to live in fellowship, community, for we are not just individuals or members of what is called today 'the nuclear family' but partners, fellow-citizens, pilgrims together. We may not always get on with one another or even like some of our fellow-travellers, but God has put us together, and calls us to love each other. This may not be easy, but it is the only way forward. So as I look towards my future I realize it is bound up by so many different strands of love, affection and responsibilities. It will be affected by circumstances, what happens to me, what happens to others, by handicaps and opportunities, disabling and enabling factors. Also I need to remember what others keep reminding me: 'You are not as young as you used to be'; and age, while it brings experience and maybe a little wisdom, also takes its toll on our chassis. I would like to think I have entered the vintage model class but I fear I may more correctly be labelled 'an old banger'. As we get older we begin to realize there are things we thought we might do we now know we will never achieve, and things dearly won we may have to let go, and that is not easy to accept – certainly I find it difficult. So back to the question I was, and am, faced with: 'Whatever next?' I found the answer made very clear for me when I was in Israel at the end of 1995. We had spent some time by the Sea of Galilee, and been able to have an hour or so on our own, and it was a very special time indeed to be free to walk by the shore, paddle in the sea, and allow all those stories from the Bible about what happened by and on the Sea of Galilee to come alive. For me, perhaps more than at any other place in the Holy Land, I felt Jesus was very near. I was caught up in the events of the past, and it was reluctantly and slowly I began to walk back up from the shore to where the bus was waiting to take us on to the next stage on our itinerary. As I passed the church facing out over the sea I noticed a plaque on the wall, one of the Praise Plaques placed there by the Evangelical Sisterhood of Mary from Darmstadt in Germany. I only stopped to look at it because I recognized what it was, for we have one on our church wall at St James' in Selby, there is another in the local park and also on Brayton Barff at the top of the hill where we hold our 'Son Rise' Service on Easter morning. They are to be found at beauty spots and holy places all over the world. This particular one by the Sea of Galilee read 'At thy word I will let down the net. Luke 5.5. The deeds and miracles of Jesus are not actions of the past. Jesus is waiting for those who are still prepared to take risks at his word, because they trust his power utterly.'

I imagine hundreds of people stop and read those words every day, people from all over the world, people just like me carried away with the beauty and the joy of the Sea of Galilee, with memories awakened of familiar stories from the Bible. But this was, I believe, a message specially for me at that moment, to go into the future assured that I would see and experience great things if only I would do as the plaque said, live dangerously, trusting in the power of the Lord.

There was no time set, no conditions offered, it was plain and simple, a matter of going on trusting and obeying, sharing the good news wherever he put me.

Can I do it? Can you do it? What if . . .? There will always be questions, always be obstacles, setbacks, times when we fall flat on our faces, but there will be the moments of sheer joy, excitement, fulfilment, the breathtaking experiences that come from sharing our lives, sharing our very selves with the Lord, who not only calls us but empowers us. Whatever next? Who knows but God? – and that surely is more than enough for anyone.

> Jesus drew near and said to them, 'I have been given all authority in heaven and on earth. Go, then, to all peoples everywhere and make them my disciples: baptize them in the name of the Father, the Son, and the Holy Spirit, and teach them to obey everything I have commanded you. And I will be with you always, to the end of the age.' (Matthew 28.18–20 GNB)

Lord, help me to say yes. (Michel Quoist)

In the name of Christ – Amen.

PLASTIC SOLDIERS, PLASTIC PEOPLE

Peter, my husband, had been busy out in the garden, cutting back the border down by the hedge and digging it over as a prelude to redesigning that end of the garden. He came into the kitchen holding a plastic model soldier in full battlekit. 'Look what I've found – another one to go with the collection.' I washed it and put it on the window sill, along with the other plastic soldiers who had come to light while Peter was digging over the patch at the back. I lined them up in formation; they certainly brought the memories flooding back. I remembered when we first moved into our house, over 26 years ago, a new house with a nightmare of a garden, full of all sorts of rubble and rubbish that had to be cleared before it began to look anything like a garden. For our small son Julian it had been a paradise, for he was devoted to his toy soldiers, and the garden was an ideal battlefield. He spent hour upon hour fighting realistic battles, covering himself and the soldiers with dust in the dry weather, and mud in the wet. The only problem was that the soldiers kept disappearing, buried below mounds of earth, and we had to keep going to the toy shop to replenish supplies to replace those who had gone 'missing presumed lost'. Now, all these years later, here they were, proving beyond a doubt that plastic does not break down, for after a wash and brush up they were as good as ever.

When Julian came in I pointed out the line of soldiers marching along the window sill. He grinned, as he lovingly handled them, then replacing them carefully on the sill he laughed and said, 'Didn't they know the war was over?'

Julian's words came back to me later that evening as I was thinking over a situation that was causing a great deal of heartache and problems in the area because of a long-running conflict between two parties, which has unfortunately spread further afield. Although many people have tried hard to bring the two parties together the situation has got worse rather than better, and the two parties are now firmly entrenched in their own hard-line position. The sad thing is that it all began years ago over a fairly simple matter, but over the years neither party would give or forgive, and so as others have taken sides it has got to a state when no one can see any way out of it. I thought of Julian's words about those long buried toy soldiers, 'Didn't they know the war was over?' You can forgive toy plastic soldiers for not knowing, but when it is grown up sensible people then it is a tragedy.

Sadly such a situation is not unique, but is far too common even within churches, with people who claim to be Christians. I have seen churches ripped apart by warring factions, and the work of ministry and mission destroyed because of just two people who take opposing views, and refuse to see any good in the other. I know it is easy to sit in judgement on others, to see their faults and at the same time be guilty of the same sin, for I have gone through times in my life when I have been so sure that I was being unjustly and unkindly treated, my views disregarded, that all I wanted to do was hit out. After all, I was in the right – or convinced I was! Every dispute seems to have two innocent parties, but we know it is not like that really, is it? Very rarely is an issue black or white; there are various shades of grey, but if we stand on our so-called dignity it leaves no room for manoeuvre, no place for reconciliation. There is an answer, which can be described in one word, forgiveness. If we have been party to a breakdown in relationships, whatever the cause, then we are both guilty and need to experience forgiveness and offer it to the other. If we are willing to acknowledge that we have sinned 'through negligence, through weakness, through our own deliberate fault', as the Alternative Service Book puts it, then we can know and share forgiveness, begin to rebuild relationships and make a new start. If, however, we hang on to our own position, feeling the other person is totally at fault, that we are the sinned against, we are incapable either of accepting forgiveness, God's or theirs, or offering it to a fellow human being, as God commands we should. We become harder and harder and finish up as hardened plastic people, with plastic personalities, stuck in our own little moulds, heartless and soulless, incapable of change.

When Jesus hung on the cross he was truly the innocent party, yet he prayed, 'Father, forgive them! They don't know what they are doing' – a prayer for us when we get ourselves into one of those stupid 'no go' situations, and shout and scream about and at others. He also taught us to pray 'Forgive us our sins as we forgive those who sin against us'. We have our part to play, for it is only when we hold out our hands in forgiveness and acceptance that we will also know the joy of being forgiven. If we have the courage and the humility to do that, then we will indeed find the war is over, and we can begin to live in peace with God, each other and ourselves, and know the victory that is God's gift for all of us.

Get rid of all bitterness, passion, and anger. No more shouting or insults, no more hateful feelings of any sort. Instead, be kind and tender-hearted to one another, and forgive one another, as God has forgiven you through Christ. (Ephesians 4.31–32 GNB)

From all arrogance and pride that makes me think
 I am always right,
from hardness of heart which causes me to be
 unforgiving and unforgiven,
from blindness to your love and compassion,
from failure to understand the needs of others,
Good Lord, deliver me.

FOUNDATIONS FOR LIFE

Mention Harrogate, and the likely response is of praise for an elegant proud town, delighting in its position set firmly in the glorious Yorkshire countryside. Its famous flower shows, its pride in being the home of 'The Great Yorkshire Show'; a town with wide horizons, space to breathe, room to play, and shops to equal the best of any fine city. Harrogate, solid, dependable, beautiful – no wonder people flock to enjoy not only the town, but the surrounding areas. Also there is the International Centre, welcoming every sort of gathering, exhibitions, trade shows and performers from all over the world. 'All roads lead to Harrogate' is true, and you are as likely to hear Japanese or German spoken, American or Australian accents in Betty's Tea Rooms as the broad Yorkshire or 'county' tones.

To be asked to speak at a conference being held at the Harrogate International Centre is an honour not to be refused, or so I thought, when asked to address the National Housing and Town Planning Councils' Conference. With the overall conference theme 'Laying the Foundations', my brief had been to address the issue of 'Laying the Moral Foundations'; but on the day, as I wandered through the Exhibition Hall, with its 'high-tech' displays, and caught snippets of earnest conversation on government policies, or financial planning, I began to wonder if anything I could say would have any bearing on their very specialized field of activity. I was well aware of why I had been asked. What the Church had to say about housing and town planning was very much in the news. The Church's initiative 'Faith in the City', begun over ten years ago, had proved to be an imaginative and adventurous undertaking, and that very week the follow-up report *Staying in the City* had been published, as well as the findings of the Church's National Housing Coalition research into homelessness. I knew also that the delegates at the conference would be of all persuasions and none, so I could hardly address them as though they were a congregation of like-minded believers. I found myself a quiet corner and went over my address. I grew more apprehensive by the minute, and wished I had never accepted the invitation. 'Why on earth do I get myself into these things?' And then I remembered what my usual reply was to such questioning: 'God opens doors, and I fall through them.' I decided that this was one of those occasions when I would fall flat on my face!

I realized this even more as I was ushered into the hall, the full glare of closed-circuit television focused on me, and then the hall plunged into darkness. I peered out into the darkness and saw nothing. Was anyone out there? If so, were they friendly, interested, hostile or what? There was no escape. I took a deep breath and began by telling the story of the two builders, the one who built on rock, and the one who built on sand, adding 'You can read it for yourself, it is part of the Sermon on the Mount in St Matthew's Gospel, which takes about ten minutes to read and a lifetime to put into operation.' I explained that Jesus was not just giving a warning about jerry-building and the need for good foundations if a building is to survive adverse conditions, but a formula for life-building, for individuals, families, communities, nations. The blueprint and the time-scale –

for immediate action. I paused, waiting for some response. Nothing. 'In for a penny, in for a pound' I decided, and went on to speak about the Ten Commandments, the code of conduct set by God for all people, for all time. Of the framework of rules which would affect every area of life: four to do with our relationship with God, six to do with family, neighbours, business colleagues, employees and strangers. 'These are commandments, not philosophical ideas.' I threw in that well-known saying, 'If God had wanted a permissive society he would have given us the ten suggestions', and went on, 'but he didn't, he gave us commandments, because he wants us to live in an integrated, caring, disciplined and loving society.' I suddenly realized I was getting feedback, the murmers from the unseen audience were warm, friendly, encouraging, and so, freed at last from my own restraints of fear and uncertainty, I launched out and shared with them how I felt about our individual responsibility before God and for each other, and of the power of God which is available for all of us if we are willing to commit ourselves to him. I spoke of the possibilities for change within each of us, and the effect this can have, on us and on others, not just now but for all eternity. I spoke of the challenge Jesus issues to us as builders of lives.

As the lights went on and I looked out into that vast area I saw the people sitting there, saw them not just as delegates to a conference, high-ranking experts in their own specialized fields, but as men and women who were struggling with the problems of life today. In families, communities, in the work situation, in the decision-making processes they were part of, and for which they were seeking sure foundations which would hold firm. I could not pretend to tell them how to do their jobs, all I could do was point them to God who would guide them, help them, share with them in every part of their lives, if they would let him.

Talking to some of them afterwards I realized a little of the enormity and complexity of the issues they had to cope with day in and day out, and I sensed a real desire by them to find firm foundations on which to base their judgement and action. I was also encouraged by the number of people who came up to me and shared something of their faith, and who applauded the decision of the conference planners to include amongst the speakers 'someone who would address the issues of faith'.

I have to confess it is not easy to take part in such gatherings; it makes me feel very vulnerable – I am outside the safety of my usual territory, I have no well-oiled pattern to resort to, I am fearful in case I get it wrong – but then the Lord calls me to follow him, to share him, and if that road leads to the Harrogate International Centre as it did that day, or anywhere else, then I need to learn to step out gladly and confidently. After all, I do not walk alone, not even on to conference platforms, whatever banner they may bear, but with the One who keeps my feet steady on the rock, Christ whom I have for ever to be my sure foundation, 'Christ, the head and corner stone' of all life and experience.

Jesus said: 'So then, anyone who hears these words of mine and obeys them is like a wise man who built his house on rock. The rain poured down, the rivers overflowed, and the wind blew hard against that house. But it did not fall, because it was built on rock. (Matthew 7.24–25 GNB)

Father,
I pray for all those in positions of responsibility in
our nation, for those who have to wrestle with the
problems of today's society, who are called upon to
make decisions which affect the lives of so many.
Give them the wisdom and the grace they need to
build their decisions and actions on the firm foundation of your word, to the glory of your name, and
for the good of all people.

'COME, YE THANKFUL PEOPLE, COME'

When does summer end and autumn begin? Is it when the strawberry fields are but a memory, and the blackberries hang heavy in the hedgerows, or could it be when we suddenly realize there is 'a bit of a nip in the air' and we decide we really must have the central-heating boiler serviced? It could be as we see the birds flying high in the sky, planning for the exodus to warmer climes as below them the fields lie bare after cereal crops have been harvested. Maybe it is the sight of sunburnt youngsters being dragged into shops which are plastered with the 'back to school' advertisements, or even when the 'Winter Sun' holiday brochures begin to look interesting, or the new railway timetables come into operation? For me it is when the notices announcing Garden Parties and Flower Festivals are replaced by those inviting one and all to come along to the Harvest Celebration, Harvest Thanksgiving, Harvest Festival, the posters often decorated with pictures of fruit and vegetables and the words 'Come ye thankful people come' in large letters, often with the added incentive 'supper afterwards'. The menu is normally the same from year to year; some specialize in cheese, wine, apple-pie and cream, while at another it may be a good old-fashioned hot-pot, but usually it consists of a vast array of cold meats, pies, sausage rolls, salad and, if the evening has turned chilly, baked potatoes, plus of course cakes, scones and trifles, all to be washed down with cups of tea. While the menu may not change the preacher usually does – it seems to give the affair an extra sparkle if a visiting preacher comes, a change of voice at least, although why is it that most harvest sermons sound the same? Maybe because there is only so much you can say, and it's all been said before, and no doubt will be said again. Harvest Services are not confined to Sundays, in fact can be held on any day of the week, no doubt fitting in with the availability of the church or village hall for the supper, and I have sometimes found myself at such services several times in one week during the height of the harvest season, Peter usually coming with me, attracted by the prospect of the supper rather than hearing the preacher yet again.

Going out to a village church in a farming area well renowned for its 'good suppers' I was amused to see that the notice on the church notice board regarding the Harvest Festival had got its priorities in the right order. Underneath the heading 'Harvest Thanksgiving' it said in very small letters: 'Service in Church 7 p.m. Special Preacher, The Revd Margaret Cundiff'. Below in large bold ones: 'Hot Supper' – it was as well!

As year succeeds to year, memories of Harvest Festivals all seem to merge into one, but some for various reasons stand out as though they happened yesterday. I well remember a late September afternoon, when the weather, which had begun as a sullen drizzle, had turned into a steady downpour, and the thick clouds and high winds made it look more like December than September. I was glad I did not have to go out that evening, for the forecast was that the weather would worsen, and there were gale warnings in operation for coastal areas. 'Pity the poor sailors' I thought as I drove home, looking forward to a quiet evening. Peter greeted me with 'You'll be getting a phone call in a few minutes, the Vicar of . . . wonders if you would preach at his Harvest Festival.' I groaned, having already done what I felt was a full complement of such services. 'When is it?' The answer came back, 'Tonight.' I looked at Peter thinking it was a joke. 'Tonight? No chance.' Peter looked anxiously at me. 'Well . . . I more or less said you would. He's been put in a difficult position, the Bishop should have been going but now he can't and everything is arranged, and I told the vicar you had had quite a lot of harvests and he said 'Good, so she will have a sermon up her sleeve . . . ' I hesitated. Peter could see I was giving in, and he went on, 'I'll come with you, and there is a supper!'

We set off to drive the fifty miles over the Wolds to the small town just a mile or two from the coast. The rain lashed down, we negotiated fallen branches, while Peter clung to the steering wheel. We arrived just in time for the service, but I saw the notices announcing the Bishop's visit still prominently displayed both outside and inside the church. I quickly robed, and 'fell in' with a very relieved vicar behind the choir. The service began and went along merrily with no mention of the change of preacher. As it got to the hymn before the sermon I nudged the large choirman on my right. 'I'm not the Bishop' I whispered. 'Aye. I 'ad noticed' he said in a gruff, rather disapproving voice. I went and preached the sermon – yes, it was one of those I had prepared earlier – and the service ended with a spirited rendering of 'We plough the fields and scatter'. We adjourned to the hall for supper. Nothing was said about the change of preacher, but I assumed that they all, like my friend in the choir, had realized there had been a change. The vicar seemed so harassed, I didn't like to mention the omission. As he saw us off he was very profuse with his thanks: 'So good of you. I just didn't know where to turn – and on such a bad night. I do appreciate it . . . ', and with that he thrust a parcel in my hand. 'Sorry about the paper, all I had in – thank you so very much –' With that he was gone, and we dashed through the puddles to get the car to drive home through the continuing gale.

'Worse things happen at sea' said Peter cheerfully, as the gale winds blew hard against the car. 'Not much' I muttered, and then remembered the parcel. I undid it to find a very splendid box of chocolates. 'What did he say about the paper?' Peter asked. 'Oh yes, he said it was all he had got.' I inspected it carefully and then laughed so much the car almost veered off the road with the impact. Between my shrieks of laughter I managed to tell him 'It says, 'Congratulations on the birth of your baby boy!'' As I said, there are some I remember quite plainly! Yet in spite of everything I love these harvest celebrations, and especially what I call the old-fashioned ones. There is something very special about people bringing what they have grown or bought and offering the best they have to God, to celebrate God's goodness in creation, to present their gifts with love to God who gave life to the seed, life to all creation, life to the world. To be reminded that 'All good gifts around us are sent from heaven above, then thank the Lord, O thank the Lord, for all his love'. To see faces aglow with excitement and happiness, to smell that unique heady perfume of fruit, flowers and vegetables, to join in singing those powerful descriptive hymns of praise to God. The traditional harvest festival, and long may it continue, reminds us of God's provision for us year by year and the need for us to play our part in providing for the needs of others out of full and grateful hearts.

Praise the Lord, my soul! O Lord, my God, how great you are! . . . From the sky you send rain on the hills, and the earth is filled with your blessings.

You make grass grow for the cattle and plants for human beings to use, so they can grow their crops and produce wine to make them happy, olive-oil to make them cheerful, and bread to give them strength . . . Praise the Lord, my soul! Praise the Lord! (Psalm 104.1, 13–15,35 GNB)

> For the fruits of his creation,
>   Thanks be to God;
> for his gift to every nation,
>   Thanks be to God;
> for the ploughing, sowing, reaping,
> silent growth while we are sleeping,
> future needs in earth's safe keeping,
>   thanks be to God.
> (F. Pratt Green)

EVA'S LAST LETTER

The postman stood on the doorstep, his usual cheery grin on his face as he handed me the pile of assorted mail. 'Quite a lot for you this morning – cheers!' – and with that he was off down the path. Quite a pile indeed, but by the look of it most of it would be soon finding its way into the wastepaper basket. 'A few more trees gone by the look of this lot' I thought as I took it through to the lounge and began to sort it out. I flipped through my bank statement, circulars, some press releases, invitations to buy, borrow, give, sign . . . a reminder about a committee meeting, the agenda for the Deanery Synod, and then a couple of personal letters. They earned priority over all the rest of the morning post. I decided the others could wait until later. I settled down to enjoy them.

The first was from a friend who had just come back from overseas, full of news, accounts of her travels, and who she had seen and what she had done. 'She does write a good letter' I thought guiltily, remembering how long it had been since I had written to her, and then it had only been a fairly brief one. I resolved to 'write a proper letter' to her later in the day, before hers got lost under that pile in my office marked 'Awaiting Reply'.

I picked up the second letter, recognizing the quavery writing on the envelope. It was from Eva, an elderly lady who had become over the last few years a sort of 'pen friend'. I had never met her, but she had written to me after she had heard me on radio, some years ago, thanking me for what I had said, and telling me how much it had meant to her. She had asked if I had a copy of the talk, as she would love to have it, so I had sent her a copy, and a letter of thanks for taking the trouble to write to me. She had written back, I replied, and so began a fairly regular correspondence. I discovered she was well into her eighties, lived alone, and could not get out very much. Her radio was a lifeline, and the voices were her friends. 'Lovely company,' she told me, 'it's just as though they are here in the house with me, so I'm never lonely.' She enjoyed poetry, funny stories, and so I would cut out of papers or magazines pieces I thought she would enjoy, and send them on to her. She in turn would send me snippets from the church magazine, and re-count the events that made up her life, the visitors she had, what the doctor had said, and any new recipes she had tried out, for in spite of her age she was still willing to try new things – 'have a go', as she put it. She was always so interested to hear of what I was doing, assuring me of her prayers and her love. It was her cheerfulness, her gratitude for everything and everybody that came over in her letters. In spite of all her restrictions she never moaned or complained, just got on with enjoying what she had, making the most of each day. It was always a joy to hear from her, so I was looking forward to reading about her latest doings as I turned the letter over to open it.

Stamped on the back of the envelope was the name and address of a firm of solicitors. 'Strange,' I thought, 'it's Eva's writing, and her usual sort of envelope, so why a solicitor's name on the back?' I slit open the envelope and took out the folded letter, just a short one from her, not the usual two or three pages. It read, 'My dear friend, this is just a short few lines to let you know that by the time you receive this note I will have passed away. I would like to thank you for our many years of lovely friendship and letters to me, I have always been so very pleased to hear from you. God bless you, and keep you safe and well. My dear love to you, Eva.'

I realized then why the solicitors' stamp on the back. She had obviously left the letter with them to be posted to me after her death so I would not be wondering why I had not heard from her, or think she had forgotten me. She had gone to all that trouble for someone she had never met, only through the radio and the post. I have to admit I shed a tear or two that morning, as I thanked God for Eva, for her friendship, her loving concern. It made me realize the value of letter writing, even of those short scribbled notes, because they can give such pleasure. Made me realize too the importance of keeping friendships alive. Life can become so busy, so hectic, it just rushes by, and it is easy for friendships to be swept away in the rushing torrents of activity, until suddenly it's too late, and we are left with regrets – 'if only'.

I cannot answer Eva's last letter, but I keep it in my letter-writing box as a permanent reminder not just of our friendship but of the value of keeping in touch while we can, for I am not aware heaven has a post code or a postal system!

I know it's an old cliché to say 'little things mean a lot', but it is true, and a letter on someone's mat tomorrow morning could make a world of difference, more than words could say. A letter from a friend is far more than mere words on paper, isn't it?

> For the joy of human love,
> Brother, sister, parent, child,
> Friends on earth and friends above,
> Pleasures pure and undefiled,
> Lord of all, to thee we raise
> This our sacrifice of praise.
> (F. S. Pierpoint)

Lord,
thank you for the gift of friends,
those who care for us, support us, encourage us;
who cheer us up, make us laugh,
understand us when we are down, wipe our tears;
friends who know us through and through,
    and love us just the same,
and even when we forget them, are always there
    for us.
God bless them, every one.

WHERE'S THE JUSTICE?

Recently in London I got caught up in a demonstration march. I didn't manage to find out what it was all about but those taking part looked very angry indeed, as they paraded with their banners up to Trafalgar Square between the lines of police. I did catch the words 'we want justice' but who for or what for I never discovered.

Justice – what is it? The dictionary puts it as 'just conduct, fairness, exercise of authority in maintenance of right, reward of virtue and punishment of vice, to treat fairly'.

In the American Declaration of Independence, Thomas Jefferson declared: 'We hold these truths to be sacred and undeniable. That all men are created equal and independent. That from the equal creation they derive rights inherent and inalienable among which are the preservation of life and liberty, and the pursuit of happiness.'

But are all men and women created equal? Have they all equal rights? Do they all receive justice? Our son works in the legal profession, and I remember him coming home one day very early on in his work at the Magistrates' Court and saying very sadly to me, 'Mum, they say all men are born equal, but they are not. I see people coming into Court who haven't a chance, because of their background, family, the area they come from. Others who've been to the right school, have the right accent, the right sort of backing, have all the advantages.' Only last week I was talking to a prison chaplain who told me she'd met a woman in prison for stealing £5 – obviously she couldn't tell me the details, but she was very concerned, and said, 'That woman should never have been taken into custody.' Yet I picked up my daily paper the same day and read of the release very early from a prison term of someone who'd defrauded thousands of people. Of course I don't know the details of why or how decisions are made, but to me it doesn't seem like justice. I look at talented young people who've never had a job, may never have a job – is that justice? I read of the so-called 'fat cats' of industry, the pay offs – is that justice? I suppose I would be told it's the economic climate – but it still doesn't answer my question.

As we look at our world we see gross injustice between nations, cultures, religions, tribes, sections of society – the haves and have nots – and it seems to me that often those who are treated badly respond by doing exactly the same to those weaker than themselves. Those sinned against become more aggressive. There seems little of 'I know what it's like to be treated unjustly, so I'll treat others less fortunate than me with compassion'. Survival of the fittest it seems to be, doesn't it? – and the fittest are not always those who are right.

The word 'justice' covers a multitude of sins – for instance the situation in the Middle East, Bosnia, Rwanda, Northern Ireland, or in our own backyard – even, dare I say it, in our own imagination and actions?

As a child I saw my parents caught up in injustice because they were poor; they were used by those who were rich, and their poverty was used like blackmail, for we lived in a tied cottage and my parents were servants in 'the big house'. I resented it, and resolved that when I grew up there would be justice for all who were oppressed. My cry was 'It isn't fair!' – to which my mother used to say 'Maybe it isn't, but you have to accept it the way it is' – to which I adamantly replied, 'I'll never accept it. It will be different, because I'll make it different!' Well, I've kept trying my best, but the world hasn't changed too much since those days, for one form of injustice replaces another, and that is because human nature has a very definite bias towards self-preservation – self-justice – whatever the cost. The real change comes about when the heart is changed, and that change can only come about when God's love fills us. From then on we have to live as Christians, and put that love into action.

St Paul, writing to his friends in Rome spells it out like this:

> Do not conform yourselves to the standards of this world, but let God transform you inwardly, by a complete change of your mind. Then you will be able to know the will of God – what is good and is pleasing to him and is perfect. (Romans 12.2–3 GNB)

As we look at the world we see so much injustice, hatred, sin, despair, and we have it hammered home day in day out. We can get, as it's been described, 'compassion fatigue'. It begins to sail over our heads – and hearts. We blot it out, it doesn't concern us, we've enough to cope with in our own lives, or we can despair of being able to do anything at all. It's all too much for us. Yet we have each been given a unique and precious gift, that of life – as Christians we have received the gift of new life – and through Christ the power of the Holy Spirit to live it, so never mind the size of the problem, the failings of others –

what are we doing with our lives? What is required of us?

We are called to be just in all our dealings, to practise justice in our daily lives, right where we are. It is a fairly simple matter to travel to London or a big city centre, wave a banner, shout, protest about injustice, but far more difficult to stick our necks out in our local community where we are known, and where our lives are plain for all to see. None of us can change the world singlehanded, but we can, by God's grace, change for the better the bit of the world where God has put us, by being fair and honest, standing up for what is right. Being just, honest and loving in our personal dealings comes first, we can go on to save the world later!

Justice has always to be tempered with mercy, and with love. Justice on its own is not enough. If I received justice, and only justice, from life, from God, from others, then I would be in a desperate situation, I would not have any grounds for hope. I know I need understanding, forgiveness, a helping hand, just as you do, we all do. It has been wisely said 'You should never look down on anyone unless you are preparing to give them a lift up' – yet how often do we condemn, look down on others, judge them?

As those who have received forgiveness, mercy and love, we are to share them with others, and in the light of this walk humbly and trustfully with God. The rest we can leave in his hands.

> The Lord has told us what is good.
> What he requires of us is this:
> to do what is just,
> to show constant love,
> and to live in humble fellowship with our God.
> (Micah 6.8 GNB)

Father,
help me to be fair and just in all my dealings, to live
my life with integrity, upholding what is right, supporting the cause of justice for all, but also preserve
me from harshness of spirit or action. Keep me always mindful of the undeserved love and mercy
which I have received from you, and which you
have called me to share with others.

THANKS TO
THE VICAR OF
DIBLEY

The hospital corridor seemed endless, and I hoped I was going in the right direction. People passed me, silent shadows, and I took little notice of them. My mind was elsewhere, on the person I was on my way to visit, my namesake, Margaret Smith. Smith was my maiden name and we were about the same age, so we often joked about being twins. We had a lot in common, the joy of family life, and the countryside, the same sense of humour and above all our faith in Christ. In the short time we had known each other we had become good friends. I felt as though I had known her all my life; we had an ease with each other, could share our feelings and thoughts in a deep personal way together. Now she was here in hospital in 'Jimmies', St James's Hospital in Leeds, a hospital renowned for its specialized treatment of so many illnesses, including Margaret's complaint, cancer, and a hospital made even more famous by the Yorkshire Television series *Jimmies*. Margaret was a fighter, but it was evident she was losing her fight against the cancer which had gripped her body. All the same, her mind and her spirit remained as bright as ever, and the times we were able to spend together were very precious indeed, so I was anxious to get to her that afternoon as soon as possible, for how many more times would I be able to be with her? Suddenly I was conscious of a figure coming very slowly towards me, a man bent almost double, wearing pyjamas and dressing-gown and leaning on a stick. It was hard to say how old he was, as his face was creased in pain, but I imagine he was in his mid to late fifties. As we drew level I said 'Hullo' and smiled at him. His face lit up with a cheeky grin and he said 'Hullo, are you the Vicar of Dibley then?' I grinned back and opened my jacket to display my clerical shirt. 'Oh, it's a giveaway, isn't it?' I said, in what I thought was a possible imitation of the actress who starred in that current series. We both laughed, and then he said 'Do you know, I've always wanted to kiss a Vicar' – so I leaned over, whispered 'What's stopping you then?' and kissed him firmly on his cheek, offering mine to him, which he responded to with a flourish.

Spotting a couple of chairs I said 'Let's sit down, shall we?' – and we sat together like two old friends. I asked him how long he'd been in 'Jimmies', what sort of treatment he was having, about his family. His face clouded over. 'They tell me they can't do any more for me, lung cancer you see. My own silly fault, smoking, drinking, doing what I shouldn't – you always think it happens to other people, not you, but . . . here I am . . . it's my own fault, but it's still hard . . .' He went on, 'I used to go to church, a long time ago, but, well, I suppose I drifted away, other things came up, and now it's too late, why should I expect God to bother with me, I've never bothered with him have I?' I put my arm round him. 'But that's where you are wrong, God is bothered about you, he loves you, he's got all the time in the world for you.' He brightened. 'Do you really think so?' We sat and chatted, and I gently shared with him what Jesus had to say to anyone who wanted to come close to him, the loving welcome that waited for them, at any time of life. He relaxed, and somehow the lines on his face seemed softer now. 'Would you like me to pray for you?' I said. 'Oh would you, I'd be so grateful.' There in the corridor I laid hands on him, prayed for him, and committed him to God's healing and loving power. We hugged each other, and then said goodbye; he went his way, and I went mine. When I got to Margaret I told her what had happened. Her eyes sparkled, and we laughed about the 'Vicar of Dibley' remarks. 'Do you think I look like the Vicar of Dibley?' I said jokingly. She looked at me and then said, 'Well, you do, really!' After a while I could see she was getting tired, so I read to her, and then prayed for her, laying hands on her as I had done for my friend in the corridor. I held her hand and said 'See you soon'. She smiled, 'Make it very soon, won't you?' I promised I would.

As I walked back down the corridor I wondered if I would see again the man I had met earlier. I realized I didn't even know his name, or which ward he was in. I could have kicked myself for not finding out – now I would never know what happened to him, where he was. But then, maybe that didn't matter. After all, God knew who he was, God loved him, and he knew it, it was between them now, no need for Margaret Cundiff to organize them. I caught sight of my own reflection as I went past the reception desk. Vicar of Dibley? – there did seem a slight resemblance, and some of her fictional experiences were very similar to some of my real-life ones. I wondered whether that man would have had the courage to say something to me had that programme not been on that week. Would we have just said 'Hullo' and passed each other by? I would never have had the opportunity to share in that conversation. I have often said God uses all sorts of people, all sorts of situations, and now I realized he can also use comedy programmes on television to bring people together, to break down barriers, open doors.

A day or two later someone at church said to me 'Margaret, have you seen that awful programme *The Vicar of Dibley* – it's terrible, it's an insult to women priests, people like you.' I smiled, thinking back to my meeting at 'Jimmies'. 'Oh, I don't know, it's quite true to life in parts – in fact someone asked me the other day if I was the Vicar of Dibley.' My friend's eyes widened in horror. 'Oh you are nothing like her, Margaret!' Then she looked at me again, and added 'Well, not much.' I laughed, 'I don't mind, it does have its advantages.' It most certainly does!

> Your speech should always be pleasant and interesting, and you should know how to give the right answer to everyone. (Colossians 4.6 GNB)

Thank you, Father, for all the opportunities you give us to share your love. Help us to realize that laughter can open many a heart, and a cheerful word can be the key that unlocks eternity.

OLD SOLDIERS
NEVER DIE

I came across the photo when I was sorting out a drawer in my office: three elderly, but very smart and mischievous-looking gentlemen, sitting together on a sofa. It was taken at a church Christmas party, for they all loved parties, and entered into them with great enthusiasm and humour. Walter, Fred and Claude. We called them 'our three old soldiers' and so they were, having all served in the First World War. Between them they had a fund of stories, sad and funny, and when they got together, there was no stopping them, reminding each other of the events of that war, 'the great war' as they always called it, and of friends who were killed then, and also who had died since. Walter, Fred and Claude were survivors, all right, and they all lived into their late eighties and nineties, and yet never seemed old, never lost their boyishness, their love of life – maybe coming so close to death had taught them to appreciate every day they had. Knowing them made us all appreciate life too – they added so much sparkle and we were so proud of them, 'our three old soldiers'. They took it in turns to lay the wreath on the War Memorial in church each Remembrance Sunday. Always immaculate, medals gleaming, backs like ramrods. Maybe at the Cenotaph in London and in great cathedrals the act would be more spectacular than that held in our ordinary down-to-earth Yorkshire parish church, but nowhere could the atmosphere have been more powerful, the sense of ceremony more obvious and the feelings, the remembering, more genuine and heartfelt. It touched each one of us, even the youngest child present, as we looked at them, as we stood with them. We shared something of how they were feeling, their pride, their sadness, their dedication. What they were, what they showed, said more than the most elequent sermon. As I recited those words by Laurence Binyon –

They shall grow not old as we that are left grow old.
Age shall not weary them, nor the years condemn.
At the going down of the sun and in the morning
We will remember them.
(Laurence Binyon, 1869–1943,
'For the fallen')

– I felt a lump in my throat, and my eyes pricking, and I felt so proud and grateful we had 'our three old soldiers'. Then Walter died, a couple of years later Fred, and finally Claude. The last time Claude, alone, laid the wreath he was in a wheelchair, but still those medals gleamed, that back was as straight as ever, and his face firm, strong, as he recalled those who had died in the trenches all those years ago, and also his two friends, Walter and Fred. We still have the same ceremony each Remembrance Sunday. We have no one who served in the First World War to lay the wreath now, but one who served throughout the Second World War, and was for part of that time a prisoner of war. He doesn't say much about his experiences, but I can tell by his face he is doing a lot of remembering, and it's hard for him, but he follows in the tradition of Walter, Fred and Claude.

Why did they do it? Become soldiers? King and Country? As their duty, out of love? I remember Walter telling me how he joined up under age. I asked him why. He told me quite simply, 'Because I had heard they got decent boots, a good coat and three meals a day' – something young Walter had not experienced until he went into the Army. He told me about the horrors of 'going over the top', how many screamed in anger, fear, pain. He said some of his young friends swore, but 'I never did, I had been brought up as a Church lad, as a Christian.' I asked him, 'Did you pray when you went over the top, Walter?' He looked very serious and far away as he thought, then he said, 'Oh yes, I prayed, I prayed hard I did.' I wondered what a young lad in the thick of battle would pray about, faced with death. Was it for survival, for his mother, for a girlfriend, for entry to heaven? I asked, 'So what did you pray for, Walter?' He looked at me, smiled and said, 'I prayed I wouldn't hit anyone. I wouldn't have liked to have killed anyone, so I fired my gun into the air.' Dear old Walter, in the midst of all that, he was concerned for other people. I don't suppose it would have gone down well with his fellow soldiers, I don't suppose he ever told them what he did, but Walter had a love for his fellow men and women that made him concerned for them, for their lives, whoever they were. He told me about a young German soldier being brought out, choking on gas. He said, 'There were our lads, and their lads, all choking, all helping each other along, and this German lad, his 'at fell off, and I picked it up for him. He said 'You keep it, a souvenir.' I looked at him, he was about my age, and I thought to myself 'Now why would I want to kill him? He's a decent sort of young feller.' I said, 'Walter, did you keep his hat?' He shook his head, 'Eh, I don't remember what happened to it, but I do remember that young feller, I hope he got home all right.' I have always remembered Walter telling me that story, and one Remembrance Sunday I shared it on radio, and got a very angry letter from a retired Army officer, who told me in no uncertain terms that Walter was a disgrace, and so was I for repeating his story! He lumped Walter and me together in the coward/traitor category, and we had a rather protracted correspondence on the subject, neither of us giving an inch! So I have not mentioned it again, until now. Looking at that photograph I am reminded of it all. I expect that young German soldier is dead by now, like Walter, Fred and Claude.

Wars have been since time began, they seem to be more brutal, more inhuman today. Perhaps because we see it all on television, we are spared none of the gruesome details, we see it happen as it happens, we see the blood, the carnage, the destruction, the horror – but do we learn? In Israel I visited the Yad Vashem, the Holocaust Memorial Museum. I could hardly bear to look, but I did, and was completely overcome with sadness and revulsion that such a thing could ever happen. I cried for those one and a half million children who suffered and died in the camps, but at the same time I know it still happens in the world. I have visited war graves in this country, and in others, and I look at the photographs of a brother-in-law I never knew who was killed serving in the RAF . . . and I say 'When will we ever learn, when will we ever learn?'

I am proud of 'our three old soldiers' and all others who have served their country, and to defend those I love I am sure I would go to war today, but I am equally proud of those who in conscience said 'no', of those who in the midst of war could still see others as human beings like themselves, and wish them no harm.

Edith Cavell said as she went to her execution, 'I realize that patriotism is not enough. I must have no hatred or bitterness towards anyone.' She paid for her

words and her actions with her life, in the steps of the
One who said as he died, 'Father, forgive them, for
they know not what they do.'

Love and faithfulness will meet;
righteousness and peace will embrace.
Human loyalty will reach up from the earth,
and God's righteousness will look down from heaven.
(Psalm 85.10–11 GNB)

Lord,
make us instruments of your peace.
Where there is hatred, let us sow love.
Where there is injury, pardon,
where there is doubt, faith,
where there is despair, hope,
where there is darkness, light,
where there is sadness, joy,
for thy mercy and thy truth's sake.
(after *St Francis of Assisi*)

'O COME YE, O COME YE, TO BETHLEHEM'

Nothing had quite prepared me for the shock wave of excitement that caused me to tingle from head to toe as we headed off the main road onto the narrower and more dusty one. It was the signpost that did it, it was marked 'Bethlehem', and I stared at it, almost in disbelief, and then the realization hit me: I was on my way to Bethlehem. In just a few minutes I would actually be there! I found myself singing a children's hymn I learned many years ago:

> How far is it to Bethlehem?
> Not very far?
> Shall we find the stable room
> Lit by a star?
> (Frances Chesterton)

The road grew bumpier, the dwellings and shops had a poor and unkempt look about them. I had the feeling of stepping back in time. Men in flowing Arab robes and traditional head-dresses, women with their heads covered, long dresses and shawls, everywhere children, darting here and there, and, watching everyone, young Israeli soldiers, guns at the ready, in armoured cars, at sentry posts on foot. My feeling of cheerful excitement was giving way to a sense of apprehension, unease.

Our bus drew up at Manger Square, our guide looked serious. 'Now be careful, watch your cameras and money. Don't get separated, keep close together, don't wander.' As we got off the bus people surged towards us, holding out postcards, wooden items, scarves, jewellery, calling to us, plucking at our sleeves. Bright-eyed children jabbered away at us, and in the shadows were the soldiers, watching. I caught the eye of one. He saw me staring at him and stiffened, his gaze a mixture of insolence, appraisal and distrust. Who could blame him? It was just days before the Israeli troops were due to pull out of Bethlehem, the PLO posters were everywhere, the celebrations already beginning. 'It must be hard to cope with being so hated, unwanted, wondering what is going to happen next,' I thought, as I looked at the soldier. He was so very young, just a teenager, doing his national service, no doubt wishing he was at home. I smiled at him, but his stare did not change. He was on duty, full alert, he could not even trust a smiling tourist. In his situation no one could be trusted – I knew the feeling as I pushed along with the rest into the Church of the Nativity, trying to keep an eye on my party, on what was going on around me and on my possessions. The church was dark and crowded, and I thought in need of a good clean. I half listened to the guide explaining the history of our surroundings. 'Now we go down into the place where Christ was born,' she said. 'Be careful, watch your heads!' A wise warning, as we ducked down into the crypt. Lamps, hangings, altars, and the most sacred spot, overlaid by the star-shaped design. I did the usual tourist thing and took a photograph, and listened to the babble of voices in many languages. No time to stare though, it was time to move on and out. As we came out again into Manger Square it was beginning to get dark, and there came the loud wailing of the 'call to prayer' from the nearby mosque. I was glad to get back into the comfort and safety of our bus.

We were all fairly subdued as we drove back into Jerusalem. No one said much, we all had our own thoughts. Was Bethlehem as I'd imagined? Maybe it was. A very ordinary place, full of noise, tension, buying and selling, pushing and shoving. It would have been like that when a very weary Mary and Joseph had arrived two thousand years ago, there because they had been ordered to go, and no doubt there were soldiers around to make sure everything was carried out as per orders. Was it the actual place? Well I suppose 'there and thereabouts' – and as for all the trappings, they are just a very human way of trying to make sense of something beyond comprehension, of God coming to earth as a baby, being born, of all places, in Bethlehem. I was glad I had been, glad I had stooped down and gone into that strange, dark old place, been reminded by that very act of stooping low of God's wonderful love for us all. Yes, God's love for the people who jostled around in Manger Square, the young soldiers, eager to be away from the place, the tourists and pilgrims from all over the world who came to look, to wonder, and all those who have lived, will live in this strange, mixed-up world of ours. I looked out of the bus window. It was dark now, but in the sky the stars were shining, shining over Bethlehem, shining over us. Quietly I sang under my breath:

> He came down to earth from Heaven
> Who is God and Lord of all,
> And his shelter was a stable,
> And His cradle was a stall;
> With the poor and mean and lowly
> Lived on earth our Saviour holy.
> (Cecil Frances Alexander, 1818–1895)

– and added, 'and he still does, he still does.'

When the angels went away from them back into heaven, the shepherds said to one another, 'Let's go to Bethlehem and see this thing that has happened, which the Lord has told us.' So they hurried off, and found Mary and Joseph and saw the baby lying in the manger. (Luke 2.15–16 GNB)

Lord,
thank you that you chose not to be born in some great stately home, but in an outhouse in an ordinary little town called Bethlehem. Thank you that you are willing to enter into our poor hearts and lives, and lift us up from earth to heaven by the power of your love.

CHRISTMAS COMES
BUT ONCE A YEAR

I had been waiting in the queue at the checkout for ages, and was lost in my own thoughts. I had just returned from a visit to Israel, my mind still full of the events out there, and to be plunged into the Christmas rush was almost a cultural shock to the system. I was brought back to the present when a voice from just behind me said crossly 'I don't know why we bother, it's just not worth it for one day.' I turned round to see a weary fellow-shopper with her trolley loaded to capacity. I did a quick side step as she was just about to ram me full on with her trolley and I smiled at her sympathetically. My smile cut no ice with her, but she did recognize a captive audience, for we were jammed before and behind with zombie-looking people clinging to their trolleys like grim death. She glared at me reproachfully. 'The car park's full, I haven't been able to get half what I came for, and they have sold out of Christmas trees.' I rushed to the defence of Christmas. 'Oh, I think it's a lovely time. Where would we be without Christmas?' The harsh reply came like a bullet out of a gun: 'A lot better off, that's what'. Suddenly the queue began to move forward, and so our conversation came to an abrupt halt as I loaded my purchases onto the moving belt. Later on I saw her, head down, going with her trolley as though she was driving in the Grand Prix. I just hoped she would not meet anyone coming in the opposite direction, for there would have been an almighty pile-up.

Having deposited my pile of shopping in the boot of my car I joined the queue to get out of the supermarket car park. It was slow work, and glancing at my fellow travellers hunched over their wheels I saw that they were feeling the strain of the Christmas rush too. As I drove home I thought of the conversation I had had, and of all the other people I had seen looking tired and weary that December afternoon. Patience exhausted, tempers frayed, purses and wallets empty and for what? I began to think of all the things I still had to do at home and for church. I too felt I was on a roller-coaster of time, and in imminent danger of flying off it. I still hadn't finished all the cards, there was the cake to ice, presents to wrap, visits to make, sermons to write and . . . Christmas . . . only a few days away. I'd never make it. Arriving home I dashed into the kitchen, started unloading my shopping, quickly turning on the oven to make sure the meal was under way, then reached out and put the radio on for it was nearly newstime – and suddenly my kitchen was filled with music, the pure clear tones of a boy soloist singing a Christmas carol.

> Love came down at Christmas,
> Love all lovely, love divine.
> Love came down at Christmas,
> Star and angels gave the sign.
> (Christina Rossetti, 1830–1894)

It was like a cold refreshing drink on a hot summer's day, I just stood there and drank it in, relaxed, enjoyed the music and the message it brought. I wished my friend at the checkout could have heard it too, but maybe she hadn't time to listen to carols, perhaps she was still in search of a Christmas tree. I hoped her temper would have improved before she got home, but then perhaps she had a lot on her plate to contend with, and not the sort of things you put through a checkout. Problems surface at Christmas just as at any other time. People can suffer through illness, tragedy, rows, worries, 365 days a year. There are no protected days, and things often seem worse around Christmas when everybody else seems to be having it easy, busy celebrating, smiling through. Being alone, in trouble, with problems, hurts, can feel a thousand times worse at Christmas; the jollity of others rubs salt in the wounds, creating bitterness, anger and a sense of frustration. I thought of her retort to my 'Where would we be without Christmas?': 'A lot better off, that's what'. Yes, maybe in a way she was right. We would have more time, less hassle, be a bit better off financially, have more space in the car park, and there would be no need for a tree, would there? There would be nothing to rush for, nothing to look forward to, nothing . . . and we would be in a helpless, hopeless state, all of us, if God hadn't decided to come to our rescue – if he hadn't sent his Son to earth to share our life, even though there was no room for him when he did come, and people said 'Go away', 'Clear off', and got rid of him – or so they thought – by nailing him to a cross when he was thirty-three. Not so many wanted to know about love, forgiveness, new life. They had too many other things to think about, to be concerned with, but he still went on loving, caring, forgiving, healing, lifting up, and in spite of everything was not defeated, but rose from the dead, so he could be with us for always, bringing those same gifts to us today. Yes, love did come down at Christmas, and stayed, and that's worth celebrating, worth everything. Like the trappings that surround the site of his birth in Bethlehem, we too surround Christmas with our baubles, our trappings – and why not? It is our way of reaching out to honour that greatest act of love, of God reaching out to us, coming down to be with us – just as long as we don't let the trappings dazzle us and so obscure the reality of God's gift, but take time to look at the star, listen to the angels, and with open hearts accept with joy and thankfulness God's gift of his Son Jesus into our lives.

There were some shepherds in that part of the country who were spending the night in the fields, taking care of their flocks. An angel of the Lord appeared to them, and the glory of the Lord shone over them. They were terribly afraid, but the angel said to them, 'Don't be afraid! I am here with good news for you, which will bring great joy to all the people. This very day in David's town your Saviour was born – Christ the Lord!' (Luke 2.8–11 GNB)

In all the busyness of Christmas, Lord, when so easily I get bogged down with the trappings and the trivia, open my eyes to see your glory shining, my ears to the message of the angels, and to realize afresh the wonder of your coming, the gift of your love to me.

CINDERS GETS IT RIGHT

The village school was buzzing with excitement as, along with parents, relatives and friends, I made my way into the rapidly filling big classroom which today had been transformed into a theatre. Children spilled over everywhere anxiously looking for their parents, with cries of 'I'm over here mum', while others in various stages of dress and undress were being organized into groups in order of performance. It was the day of the Christmas show, a day not to be missed as the children put on their annual concert just before Christmas. No first night at Drury Lane could equal the sense of exhilaration and anticipation as performers and audience alike awaited 'curtain up'. We, the audience, glued together like sardines in a tin, were hunched on plain wooden chairs that certainly bore no resemblance to the plush seats of the Theatre Royal, York, but that didn't matter. We were in for 'a good do', for we all knew by experience this was one of the highlights of the village year. As I looked round I recognized many of the young mums and dads. They had themselves been taking part in similar shows just a few years back, and I thought to myself 'How many years have I been coming here?' – realizing with a shock it was over 20 – how time does fly when you are having fun! And it's certainly fun being part of Wistow School, sharing not just in the Friday morning assemblies but in the life of the school throughout the years. But no more time for memories, it was time to enjoy this year's production, and to enter the world of fairyland, the story of *Cinderella*.

It was a fantastic show, the children were brilliant, real pros, all of them, word perfect, and the costumes and staging would have done justice to any theatre – but then they couldn't go wrong. We all knew by heart the story of *Cinderella*, that in the end poor little Cinders would marry the handsome Prince Charming and they would live happily ever after, so we all were ready for the grand finale. But the Wistow School production had a twist in the tail. Cinders turned Prince Charming down. She told him firmly that she wasn't interested in Princes, palaces or crowns, and that she was going to marry her faithful friend Buttons who had always cared for her and supported her even when she was in rags in the kitchen. That was true love, that's where her happiness was to be found – and with that she went off arm in arm with Buttons, leaving Prince Charming to the mercy of the ugliest ugly sister. We all cheered, the children bowed, and a good time was had by all – another very successful production to go down in the school records, and a tribute to the hard-working teachers and helpers too, who had enabled the children to give of their very best, and given us something to 'think on' too, to ponder on as we made our way home that cold and drizzly December afternoon. For there is something in us all that yearns for fairy-tale endings in our lives. We get dazzled by the seemingly glittering prizes of life. If only we had a fast car, the mini-mansion, the body beautiful and the right numbers on Saturday night in the National Lottery, then we would be really and truly and wonderfully happy – but would we? Surely happiness comes from knowing that we are loved for ourselves, not for what we have got. It is about sharing good times and bad, laughter and tears, on the hard chairs of life as well as the plush seats at the front. Knowing the security of being part of a family or community, knowing friendship, neighbourliness, acceptance. Prince (or Princess) Charming may be fun for an afternoon, but it's the Buttons of life, who don't make a song and dance about what they do, that make the difference. 'Salt of the earth', 'spice of life', 'solid as a rock' folk, that's them, and blessed are we when we have such as friends, and blessed are we too when we can be that sort of a friend to others. When Jesus chose his friends, those he wanted to share his life with, those he would entrust his message to, he went to ordinary working men living very ordinary sorts of lives, because he recognized their worth as people, even though most others wouldn't have given them a second glance. A good judge of character was Jesus – still is!

> Jesus said: 'My commandment is this: love one another, just as I love you. The greatest love a person can have for his friends is to give his life for them.' (John 15.12–13 GNB)

Thank you, Lord, for all those whose love and friendship, support and counsel enrich my life day by day; those who go on loving me even when I'm downright difficult and unloving; who stick by me through thick and thin, whatever others may think or do. As I have received so much from others, help me to give freely too.

DID YOU SEE . . . ¿

The police spokesman stood with his back to the carnage of mangled cars and lorries. In the background were firemen, ambulance crews, police moving around, flashing lights, lifting gear, the whine of sirens, the pictures telling the story of the horrific motorway crash. 'It's the usual story I'm afraid,' he said, 'people going too fast, travelling too close in bad conditions, and this is the result.' The background was then brought into centre focus, allowing the full horror to be revealed, and then the policeman stared into the camera, and with an expression born of exasperation coupled with fatigue said fiercely, '. . . and our rescue work is being greatly hampered by people stopping to gape. We've had such a number of cars stopping on the other side of the carriageway there have been further accidents, and some of our rescue crews have been unable to get through . . . please, please, stay away.'

How I agreed with him. Who were these people who were so insensitive, so unfeeling, as to watch a tragedy like that, as though it was a circus, a show, put on for their entertainment? I felt so angry – sitting there in my comfortable armchair in the lounge, watching the six o'clock news. Then suddenly, like a bolt, it hit me. I was guilty too. I had heard about the pile up as I drove home from town, and had immediately switched on the television to see what was happening, pausing only to make myself a cup of coffee to enjoy while I watched the news. All right, I had not dashed along the M1 but I was still part of the gaping

130

crowd, a crowd of millions. We all do it daily, don't we? Why is it that bad news, tragedy, disasters, sell papers, make us rush to turn on our radios and televisions? What is it within us that compels us to stand and stare, to thrust ourselves into the scene? Why is it that good news rarely makes the front pages, or even the middle to back ones? It is no use blaming editors, reporters, photographers – it is a matter of what the public, which means you and me, want. The media is a business, a vast empire of businesses, dependent on sales, ratings, viewing figures, dependent on our support. Through the volume and variety offered by the media we have become what in modern terms are described as 'couch potatoes'. Life is brought into our living-rooms, kitchens, bedrooms, even the bathrooms. Living life to the full, taking part actively, requires so much effort, why bother? After all, we can view it in comfort, without moving a muscle. Life has become a spectator sport, a one-way activity.

We may decry this in others, but let us be honest. We are in danger, whoever we are, however good our intentions, of being sucked into it all. How many important meetings are poorly attended because 'Well, it's *Coronation Street* on tonight. . . *The Bill* . . . *East-Enders* . . .' Sunday evening churchgoing has never recovered from the popular *Forsythe Saga* television series of some years ago, and the *Radio Times* is consulted before any arrangements are made to be absent from home. The advent of the video just means we spend more time watching, catching up on the other channels, and, yes, I do it too!

No longer people of independent thought, but readers, listeners and viewers. Yet surely that is allowing the media to use us rather than seeing the media as a wonderful tool, a window on the world, a means of information, to stretch our minds and imagination.

After all, the prime aim is to inform, educate and entertain – a good diet, if kept to – but then having received all this, what do we do with it? How do we sort out the good from the bad? If we want to be spiritual people, more God-centred, then should we not throw out the radio and television, cancel the papers and just read the Bible, worthy literature, John Wesley's sermons or the Thirty-Nine Articles of Religion? A story I heard many years ago has remained with me. A young kitchen maid who worked in 'the big house', working hard from morning to night, with very little time to herself, and with certainly no outside pursuits bar a visit home on rare occasions, asked if she might have the daily newspaper to take with her to bed when it had been finished with. It was not one of the lively 'easy read' newspapers we are accustomed to today, but a very serious newspaper in the true sense of the word 'news'. Her employer was intrigued to know what she did with it, what interested her so much. So one day he asked her, 'What do you find so interesting in the newspaper?' The girl smiled at him. 'Well sir, I read the births, marriages and deaths. I pray for all those babies who have just come into the world, that they will grow up strong and happy and bring and give love to their families. I pray for those who have got married, that they will be faithful to one another and grow in love, and their homes might be full of peace and joy. I pray for those who are sad because they have lost a loved one, and I pray God will comfort them, give them peace and hope in their trouble, that they will know his arms supporting them to bring them through.'

Ever since I heard that story I try to do the same each day as I read my newspapers. As I watch and hear the news, I try to lift those situations, the people caught up in them, into the presence of God, for I

believe prayer reaches out and touches anyone, anywhere, including people for whom maybe no one else
prays. Who knows the result our prayer might bring?
That cry to God on another's behalf? Through the
media we are given a window on the world, sometimes a very distorting window, but we see people,
often in dire situations, as we look through that window. If we only stand and stare, go 'tut tut . . . how
dreadful . . .' are we any better than those who stand
and stare, on the side of motorways, outside victims'
of tragedies homes, on courtroom steps? Those faces
staring out at us from newspapers, television screens,
the situations reported – however dreadful, whatever
is involved, what can we do, if anything, to help? By
our prayers, our genuine concern, we can reach out
and touch them. In the words of Lord Tennyson,
'More things are wrought by prayer than this world
dreams of.' We may never fully comprehend the
power of prayer, but what we are called to do is practise it, with love.

> Do all this in prayer, asking for God's help. Pray on
> every occasion, as the Spirit leads. For this reason
> keep alert and never give up. (Ephesians 6.18 GNB)

Father,
I pray for all those who are in the news today, in
their success or failure, joy or tragedy; through
what they have done or said, or what has been done
to them or said about them. You love them, they are
your children; may they know that. Be with them
now and in the days ahead. In Jesus' name I ask it.

BE PREPARED

Travelling in the rush hour on the London Underground I found myself eye level to an advertisement for a further education course. It read, 'You can't predict the future, but you can prepare for it.' I can't remember now what or where the course was, but I certainly remember that very catchy phrase. It was one of those little sayings which go round and round in the mind, and certainly in mine, as I had been thinking about the future, all the endless possibilities, probably something to do with all those calendars, diaries, file inserts, which are so prominently displayed on sale at the approach of a new year. I know changing just a digit doesn't really make any difference, but it does sharpen the mind, and I had been wondering what the new year would bring for me and my family, for those around, our country, the world. One thing for sure, there would be plenty of surprises ahead, and I didn't dare suppose all of them would be pleasant, judging on past years, although, always the optimist, I look forward with eager anticipation to discovering and experiencing what lies ahead. Life is full of changes, that is for certain, and as the advertisement so rightly said, 'You can't predict the future . . .' There are far too many variables to do that, but what about that second part – '. . . but you can prepare for it'? Did it mean isolate yourself from any possibility of change, be double wrapped against disaster, go and live on a desert island? I think, having read the small print on that advertisement, they were suggesting we improve our knowledge, with their help, so as to be more able to cope with whatever life throws at us. I reckon it is very good advice, for we all need to be made aware of what is happening in our world, to try and understand it, and be able to use the latest technology. After all, even five-year-olds are 'computer-literate' these days, and it's a case of 'if you can't beat 'em, join 'em'. So, it made me wonder whether I should get myself enrolled on a computer course, get to grips with hardware and software and discover how to chase that 'mouse' around. I have the jargon even though I am very confused about its meaning. But life is more than technology, it is about relationships – how we get on with other people. Do we take time to find out what makes them tick? Why they react the way they do? What triggers them off? It could save a lot of problems and misunderstandings if we did. Then what about ourselves? Often we don't want to know the truth about ourselves, so we close our eyes and minds, and then wonder why we get ourselves into such a mess – I know I do.

Then what about God? Where does he come in – or does he? It is said most people claim to believe in God, at times pray to him, but is it a case of just seeing him as a panic button to be pressed in dire emergency? That tube advertisement certainly made me ponder on all these things, take stock of my present life, my attitudes and reactions. Looking back over the years I have already enjoyed, I know I have got to know God better through prayer, study, worship, friendship with other Christians. I have learned by experience to make God my first call at all times. After all, he is my best friend. My confidence in him has been built up by experience, and that means everything as I look forward to whatever life has in store.

All our relationships with other people, ourselves and God need to be kept in good repair, the lines open.

Of course it takes time, effort and love, but it's worth it – well, I have found it so. It is true we cannot predict the future, not even today, leave alone tomorrow, next week, next year, but we can be prepared for it by knowing who we can turn to, that God is there already. Past, present, future, all in his good hands, and we are in his – for always.

Your constant love is better than life itself,
and so I will praise you.
I will give you thanks as long as I live;
I will raise my hands to you in prayer.
My soul will feast and be satisfied,
and I will sing glad songs of praise to you.
As I lie in bed I remember you;
all night long I think of you,
because you have always been my help.
In the shadow of your wings I sing for joy.
I cling to you,
and your hand keeps me safe.
(Psalm 63.3–8 GNB)

Lord,
I find the thought of tomorrow both exciting and
frightening.
What will happen? Will I be able to cope?
Yet you have never failed me in the past,
you have given me the gift of this day,
and I know that in that strange unknown place I call
'tomorrow' you are already there, waiting to draw me
into the safekeeping of your love.

136

NEVER GIVE UP

I knocked on the door and waited . . . and waited . . . and waited. I tried again, still no reply. 'Strange,' I thought. Alice knew I was coming, in fact had told me in no uncertain terms what time she was expecting me, and I knew better than turn up at the wrong time. I looked through the window. The fire was on, the daily paper on the sofa and through the open door into the kitchen I could see her. I went round the back and knocked – still no reply. As I looked through the kitchen window, I saw a flash of someone darting into the living-room. 'She's playing games with me again,' I decided, for it was not the first time it had happened to me, or other visitors from church, so I banged again and then opened the back door and called her. Red-faced she turned on me. 'You could have killed me, frightening me like that,' she said accusingly. 'I could have had a heart attack.' I apologized, explaining I had told her I was coming – in fact she had fixed the time, and so here I was, and how pleased I was to see her. It was obviously not a mutual pleasure. 'Well, I can't be doing with you, and I don't want any of that.' She pointed to my Communion kit. 'I'm not in the mood, I've gone off Church. Look at the state of the world, and what does God do about it – nothing. I'm fed up with him, and the Church, and everybody. Anyway,' she added defiantly, 'I've lost my faith, and I've lost my purse as well.' I put my arm round her. 'Come on now, sit down, let's have a think, where did you put your purse? When did you last have it?' She went on muttering, and then exclaimed 'Oh, it's here. Well, I didn't put it here.' She glared at me, as though I had moved it. 'Right then, now you've found your purse, sit down a minute, we could have a prayer together.' 'I've told you, I'm not in the mood, I don't want to hear about God today thank you.' I gently took her hand, and prayed for her, for peace, for strength, for her to know God's love surrounding her. Then I left her. I knew we were not going to get anywhere that morning. She had times like that when whoever turned up got the rough end of her tongue, yet she couldn't help it, she was frustrated with herself. Always a very independent woman, she found increasing age a wearisome thing, and her biggest fear was she would 'land up in a home, and I don't want it'.

The next time I went there was no mention of my previous visit, although she did complain about the way God was looking after her. 'It's about time he did a bit more. I thought you said he loved me – I haven't seen any of it.'

There are some visits I make, although not in 'fear and trembling' but still with a degree of caution, wondering what I am going to find, and I feel I need to throw my hat in first – as a good old saying puts it. It can be disheartening, but afterwards I can often see the funny side of some of the remarks I get, and I do realize that sometimes people vent their feelings on ministers because they know we will still go on caring about them. They trust us enough to shout at us, and maybe that is a compliment. Recounting my story of the visit at our 'Ministers' Fraternal Meeting' – our monthly get-together, over a lunchtime, of local ministers and clergy, I found everyone had an even worse horror story to tell – mine was quite mild compared with some of the others. It was a great comfort, in a strange sort of way, to know we are all in the same boat, and of course the happy visits outweigh the difficult ones a thousandfold.

A couple of days after my fraught visit I was with some friends who have a farm in the village and naturally had to meet all the animals, including the latest arrivals. They all have names, and I especially like Rupert, the boar, a very friendly and very large gentleman pig. We were discussing animals' names and how they got them, and the farmer's little girl piped up, 'We had Grumpy, didn't we, dad?' Ian, her dad, told me the story of Grumpy, a rather bad-tempered animal who was now no longer to be seen. Amanda said very confidentially, 'We called him Grumpy because he was grumpy, we didn't like him, so we ate him.' I laughed and Ian teasingly said to me, 'And what are you laughing at then?' I told him that maybe I had just discovered the answer to a problem I sometimes had with those who should be nameless. On reflection I decided maybe that was the trouble with some people: they get so eaten up with worries, by feeling rejected, cast on one side, useless, that they react in the way they do as a means of a self-defence, snapping and biting even at a hand held out in friendship or help. Crying out for help inside, they are unable to express that need, and it becomes a vicious circle. Unless that circle is broken, the situation hardens, and the only way to break the circle is go on holding out the hand of friendship, taking the flak until the message gets through. It takes time, a long time with some people; there are setbacks, often they retreat again and again into themselves, their pains and troubles, but then we can only stand by them, physically by our presence, or by our prayers. Maybe that seems so little, our tiny efforts and our prayers so seemingly ineffectual, and there is a temptation to give up; but as Mother Teresa said, 'In this life we cannot do great things, we can only do small things with great love.' Whatever happens we should never give up on people, for after all,

God never gives up on us, does he? And for me that is the greatest incentive I know even for the grumpiest of grumpies!

> This is what love is: it is not that we have loved God, but that he loved us and sent his Son to be the means by which our sins are forgiven. Dear friends, if this is how God loved us, then we should love one another. (1 John 4.10–11 GNB)

Lord,
give me understanding,
give me patience,
give me love.

LIFE IS CHANGING

Northerners have often been accused of being 'tight' where money is concerned. As someone who has spent most of her life in the north I see that as a compliment, but prefer to rephrase it as being 'careful'. Northerners, I have found, are extremely generous, but they do like a bargain, and if there is 'owt for nowt' that is even better – which is my position, as an adopted Yorkshire-woman. So I am a great collector of coupons, free offers and giveaways, including that of a bright blue spongy ball which sits on my study window. I picked it up at a Money Show, along with various pens, stickers, key-rings and other odd but useful items. It seemed a strange thing for an insurance company to be giving away, so I asked what it was for. The young man on the stand explained it was 'a worry ball'. If you played with it, squeezed it in your hand, it would help relieve your worries and was something no one could afford to be without in this day and age. Written across it were the words, 'Life is changing', plus of course the name and telephone number of the insurance company to contact, if your worries about life changing get too much for you. So I am the proud possessor of a worry ball, which does give an air of cheerfulness to my study, and some-times when stuck for words I give it a friendly squeeze; but it's the words on it which intrigue me: 'Life is changing'. Well of course no one would disagree with that statement, but is it meant to imply life is changing for the worse, and so I should be worried, and make sure I protect myself, or could it be life is changing for the better, and I can relax?

As I look around society, my own community, I see much has changed, is changing for the worse. The decline of law and order, the rise in vandalism, aggression, drug-taking and pornography. The breakdown of family life, of decent standards of morality, the widespread ignorance and apathy concerning the Christian faith, the failure of the Church to influence society and individuals, the problems of the Monarchy, the powerlessness of the state to govern effectively – the list is endless, and I would also add two of my own particular great sadnesses: the loss of Sunday as a special day set aside for God, for rest, a day that is different; and the rise to power of that great monster, the National Lottery, spawned by a morally bankrupt society.

Yet I can also see, and appreciate, much that has changed for the better. The strides in medical and scientific knowledge which have been life-saving for so many, helping combat disease and suffering. Our horizons have been widened by technology, we are indeed 'a global village', and knowing the need has often resulted in immediate help being given, for instance in the Ethiopian famine, and in many other parts of the world where disaster has struck. We have so much choice – take a look at the shelves in the local supermarket, and think back only a few years to what was available. There are more opportunities to learn new skills, whatever your age; communication and travel is so simple – for instance, where would we be without the telephone, the motorways or highspeed trains?

It is so easy to harp on about 'the good old days' and forget to count our blessings in our present state. We need to take the challenges and opportunities we are given and use them wisely and well as good stewards.

Life is all about change: we begin to change from the moment we are conceived; we grow, we develop, in body, mind and spirit. The natural world we live in is continually changing. The tides ebb and flow, the sun rises and sets, the seasons succeed from one to another, and we are changed by time if nothing else! We cannot press a pause button and hold the world and ourselves in a state of suspension, like a game of 'statues'. The tape plays on, and we go on. So life IS changing. What do I do? Sit and play with my worry ball, or what? The good news of Jesus Christ is all about change, the possibility of change, the challenge of change, the invitation to change. He invites us to come to him, and let him change us, to give us a new life, a new heart, a new direction, a new hope. To be converted means to be turned round, to change direction from going our way, the world's way, to going God's way, the way that leads to life. This is not a once and for all change – although for many it begins in a very dramatic way, for others it is very gradual and gentle. It means being open to God, to what he is saying, and allowing the Holy Spirit to work within us, not just to change us, but so we might be agents of change for the good in life, in society. It was Cardinal Newman who wrote those very wise and perceptive words, 'Here below to live is to change, and to be perfect is to have changed often.' We do not need to fear change, because as we entrust ourselves to God we have the security to cope with and to effect change. We have stability in the promise 'I am the Lord and I do not change' (Malachi 3.6 GNB), and in Hebrews 13.8 we are assured 'Jesus Christ is the same, yesterday, today and forever.' What more do we need? Whatever comes, we can look the world straight in the eye, and take up the challenges to live out our Christian faith unafraid amid change, to have the confidence to keep our Christian integrity, to be unashamed, and to oppose evil and work for good where we are, where God has put us, right now.

Serving a changeless Christ in a changing world, I can smile at my bright blue worry ball, can applaud its message, 'Life is changing', and praise God in the words of Charles Wesley:

> Finish then thy new creation,
> Pure and spotless let us be;
> Let us see thy great salvation,
> Perfectly restored in thee.
>
> Changed from glory into glory,
> Till in heaven we take our place,
> Till we cast our crowns before thee,
> Lost in wonder, love and praise.
> (Charles Wesley, 1707–1788,
> 'Love divine')

I ask that your minds may be open to see his light, so that you will know what is the hope to which he has called you, how rich are the wonderful blessings he promises his people, and how very great is his power at work in us who believe. (Ephesians 1.18–19 GNB)

Almighty God,
who alone can bring order
to the unruly wills and passions of sinful men:
give us grace,
   to love what you command,
   and to desire what you promise,
that in all the changes and chances of this world,
our hearts may surely there be fixed
where lasting joys are to be found;
through Jesus Christ our Lord.
(Collect for the fourth Sunday after Easter,
from *The Alternative Service Book 1980*,
copyright © The Central Board of Finance
of the Church of England)

GOOD ENOUGH FOR GOD
Anne Townsend

This book explores the ways in which we can seek healing of emotional hurts and scars from the past, freeing us to find a deeper, truer faith and closer relationship with our Creator. 'Here is a book that will help you come to terms with yourself – your real self.'
Roy Williamson, Bishop of Southwark

FAITH IN DARK PLACES

Combining moving stories from the inner city with a fresh approach to the gospel, David Rhodes explores the revolutionary idea that the good news of God's love is being spoken to a tired and damaged world by those rejected as worthless: the homeless and the poor.

THE LORD AND HIS PRAYER
Tom Wright

This small masterpiece of a book contains a great deal to stimulate and refresh both the mind and the heart. Phrase by phrase, the author demonstrates how a true understanding of the Lord's Prayer can be the starting-point for a rekindling of Christian spirituality and the life of prayer.

THE HEALING POWER OF PRAYER
Bridget Meehan

'This book rings with confidence that Jesus has power today to heal us spiritually, physically and emotionally. Above all, it is a practical book, offering forms of imaginative prayer which can be used to receive Christ's healing either alone, or in groups.' Graham Dow, Bishop of Willesden.

Also available from Triangle

TAPESTRY OF VOICES
Meditations on women's lives

Michele Guinness compiled this unique book to bring together different insights into the experience of women. Writing many of the pieces herself and commissioning new reflections from others, she explores the varied stages in every woman's life.

MADE FOR EACH OTHER
Reflections on the Opposite Sex

Drawing on the work of writers well-known and not so well-known, Michele Guinness has created a delightful and at times frank compilation which explores the ambivalent feelings we all have about the opposite sex, acknowledging that 'the world needs us both, and without one another it would be a much drearier, if less complicated, place.'

THE WINTER IS PAST
A true love story which burst the bounds of the cloister

He was an abbot, bound to his monastery by life vows. She was a novice nun, struggling to curb her independent spirit and come to terms with living in a convent. In this book, Helen Weston tells her story of a love which brought unlooked-for joy and sorrow to the people caught up in it.

SOME DAY I'M GOING TO FLY
Hilary McDowell

Disabled from birth seven times over, the author tells, in prose and poetry, stories from her remarkable life. Hers is the voice of a unique personality, combining a warm sense of humour with a moving message of hope and faith in God's enabling power.

Also available from Triangle

LANDSCAPES OF GLORY
An English Pilgrimage

A magical, mystery journey by Tom Davies, an award-winning writer and professional pilgrim who, one long hot summer, set out to track down the soul of England and discover the true state of the country's spiritual health. It is a powerful call on God by a Celtic heart and a poetic and funny meditation on the joys of the ordinary world by a man who can bring even the smallest details into vivid life.

A CONTINENT CALLED PALESTINE
One Woman's Story

This is the remarkable account of Najwa Kawar Farah's life: growing up as a Palestinian Christian in Nazareth, enduring the founding of the state of Israel, living as an exile in what had been her homeland. It offers a unique insight into the hearts of the world's oldest – and often forgotten – Christian community, the believers who trace their faith directly back to New Testament times.

A TIDE THAT SINGS
The Story of a Vocation

This classic book tells the story of 'divine coincidences' which brought Sister Agnes to the remote Shetland island of Fetlar, to live a life of prayer and hard work, giving herself to poverty and simplicity and discovering many spiritual riches along the way.

Triangle Books
can be obtained from all good bookshops.
In case of difficulty, or for a complete list of our books,
contact:
SPCK Mail Order
36 Steep Hill
Lincoln
LN2 1LU
(Tel: 01522 527486)

Or phone 0345 626747 (all calls charged at local rate).